CW01642732

THE STREET CHARACTERS OF A VICTORIAN CITY

John Sowden's Bradford

For my wife
Jackie

THE STREET CHARACTERS OF A VICTORIAN CITY

John Sowden's Bradford

Paintings by John Sowden
Text by Dr Gary Firth

ARTS, MUSEUMS AND LIBRARIES DIVISION
CITY OF BRADFORD METROPOLITAN COUNCIL

Published by the Arts, Museums and Libraries
Division of Bradford Metropolitan Council
Central Library
Prince's Way
Bradford
West Yorkshire
England
BD1 1NN

First published 1993

Text © copyright Dr Gary Firth
Paintings © copyright Bradford Arts, Museums and Libraries

ISBN 0 907734 40 5

Printed by Amadeus Press Ltd, 517 Leeds Road, Huddersfield
Typeset in Palatino by Highlight Type Bureau Ltd, 31 Briggate, Shipley.

CONTENTS

ILLUSTRATIONS

PHOTO CREDITS

The White Swan Inn – Bradford Art Galleries and Museums
The Swan Arcade – M. Bruce (Bradford Photographic Survey) and Bradford Libraries
1, Blenheim Road – Bradford Libraries
The Mechanics' Institute – Bradford Libraries

The entries from the diaries of John Sowden are provided courtesy of West Yorkshire Archive Service, Bradford District Archives.

THE PAINTINGS

ACKNOWLEDGEMENTS

Having read Edith Holden's *Country Diary of an Edwardian Lady* in 1977, and knowing of the existence of Sowden's character paintings since my childhood visits to Bolling Hall, I toyed with the idea of writing *The Urban Sketchpad of a Victorian Gentleman*, but several publishing houses were not easily convinced of this brilliant and intuitive concept. Therefore I must reserve my major thanks to Paul Lawson and John Triffitt of Bradford's Arts, Museums and Libraries Service for their belief in the project and for their encouragement and support throughout.

I owe a particular debt of gratitude to Anthea Bickley, Senior Keeper (History) at Bolling Hall, whose knowledge of local and social history I have drawn upon for twenty years or more. Through Anthea Bickley, I should like to thank Bradford Museums and Art Galleries for permission to reproduce the paintings in this book. I am also indebted to the West Yorkshire Archive Service in Bradford for permission to reproduce from the Sowden diaries and in particular, to Ian Mason for his help with archive materials. I should also like to acknowledge the Bradford Antiquarian Society for its help and encouragement over many years.

Finally Bob Duckett of Bradford's Reference Library has been constructively helpful in the final stages before publication; my thanks also to Jean Endicott for the secretarial work.

Gary Firth,
Wilsden
June 1993

THE SOWDEN WATERCOLOURS

John Sowden was a local man and an artist. He taught art for most of his life, and painted too. His works were mostly watercolours, though he also did a small number of oils. His preferred subjects seem to have been landscapes. In the early 1880s he began, purely for his own private pleasure, to paint a series of small watercolour portraits of prominent personages in Bradford, the "Worthies" and the "Characters", the latter being mostly street traders. Of the "Worthies" it is noticeable that some prominent personages are not in the series; rumour says that he would not approach people of whom he disapproved, usually because of their political or religious opinions, and that there were also people who refused his invitation to "sit". It would be interesting to know which party was to blame for any gaps, particularly as a wide range of opinions are represented in the opus! The street characters were all "respectable": he would not paint any others.

The series eventually contained 358 portraits, some of them unfinished and/or unattributed, these latter dating from the years 1911 to 1914, by which time Sowden was an old man. In 1921 he gave the whole collection to the Museum, a most generous and delightful gift. With them we also have a series of exercise books which contain biographical notes about the "Worthies", but not the "Characters". We do not know the source of the information in them so we cannot vouch for their accuracy, although they appear to be in Mr Sowden's hand. They were obviously written some time after about 1915, and not at the same time as the portraits were painted.

Watercolours are fragile and suffer badly from being exposed to daylight. Many of them are already seriously faded. In the interests of their continued preservation we can therefore only put small selections on display occasionally; they are too precious to be treated cavalierly. They can, however, be seen by prior arrangement, and photographed for private records. Application should be made to Bolling Hall Museum, Bowling Hall Road, Bradford BD4 7LP.

Anthea Bickley
Senior Keeper (History)
Bolling Hall Museum
Bradford

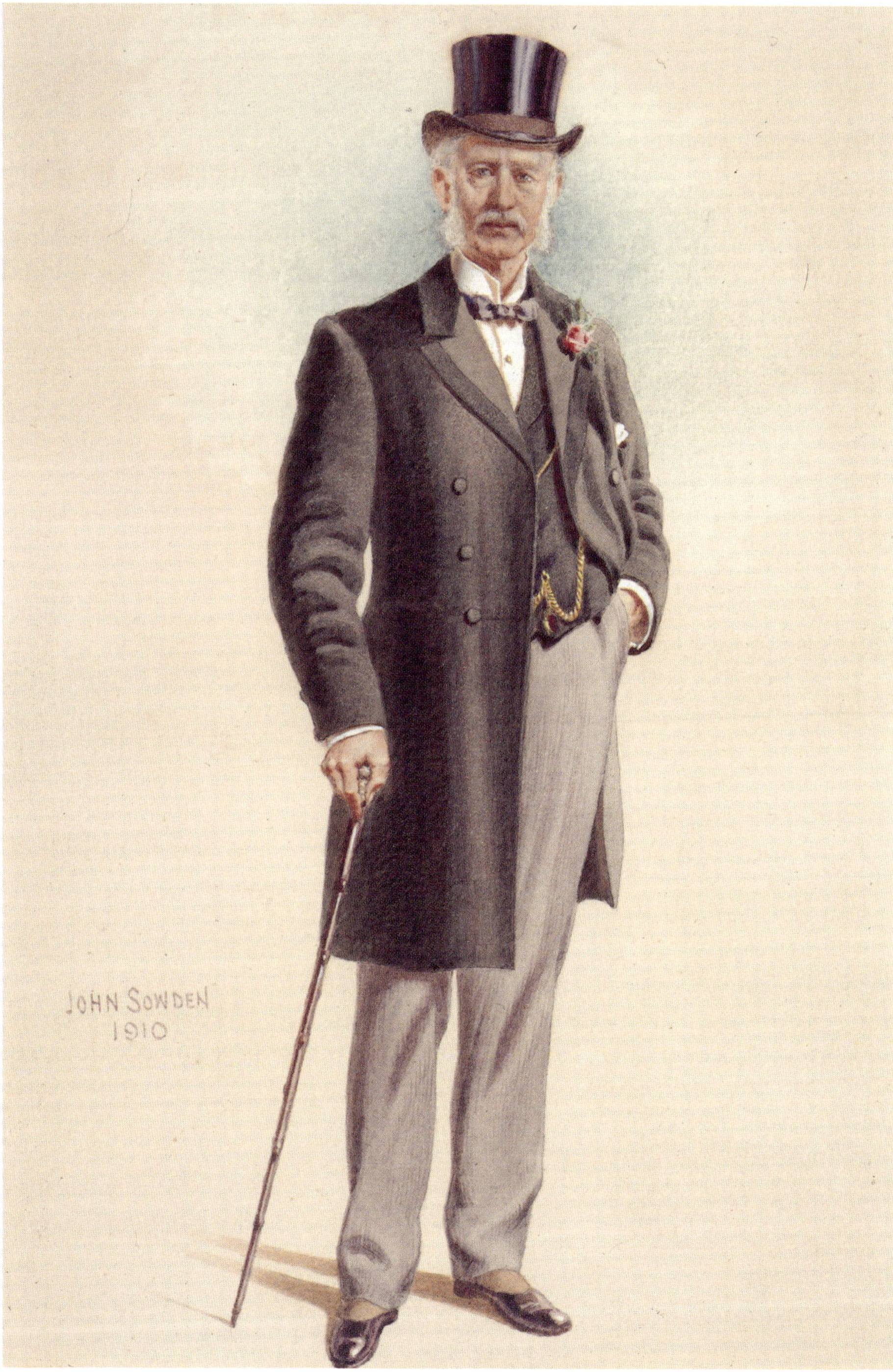
JOHN SOWDEN
1910

JOHN SOWDEN

When he died in 1926 John Sowden's erect and well groomed figure was one of the most familiar to the people of Bradford. He had, in fact, become one of the most outstanding and celebrated of the Bradford characters whom he loved to paint.

He had been born in 1838 only a year after the accession of Queen Victoria, the son of William and Mary Sowden. His father was a self employed joiner who had combined with others of his class to form a housing club and build houses in the Vicar Lane area of Bradford. The Sowden home at No. 16 Ebenezer Street gave his parents the chance of social improvement and the potential for a place in the lower middle class, home ownership being an important criterion of early Victorian middle-class status. The young Sowden grew up in a town that was fast becoming a world centre for worsted textile production. This growth was achieved at tremendous social cost. Bradford's population had rocketed from 43,527 in 1831 to 103,778 in 1851. By the 1840s the town was badly regulated, the original authority systems being unable to cope with serious problems in public health and public order which the massive numbers of immigrants had created. John Sowden's early artistic talents were quickly put to work when, as a teenager, he was articled into the profession of architect in the practice of George Knowles where there was every reason to believe Sowden would do well but for the fact that he was determined upon a career as a professional artist.

By the middle of the nineteenth century William Sowden had become a substantial property owner and developer and could afford to indulge and encourage his son's artistic aspirations, simultaneously warning the boy that he should earn his own living and not depend upon a private income. By 1855 John Sowden had joined the evening art classes of the Bradford

Mechanics' Institute, which had been founded in 1832 to propagate the ideology of self-help and self improvement amongst the respectable working men of the town. In 1858 he was a prize pupil there and in the very year of his graduation J. V. Godwin, a local worsted merchant and governor of the Institute, addressed the Social Science Association thus:

> *Those who have watched the Bradford Mechanics' Institute are able to state that there have been year after year an unbroken stream of youths, sons of working men rising to positions of responsibility which in all probability they never would have filled without its aid, and in many cases entering upon and pursuing a successful middle class career by the habits, the knowledge and the connections acquired in the Institute.*

Words most appropriate to young Sowden's position for, within a year of his graduation, he had replaced James Lobley as the art master of the Institute, a post which he was to hold until 1901. Furthermore, Sowden was also appointed as second master of the Bradford School of Design about this time. By the early 1860s, Sowden had also set himself up as a professional artist and landscape painter in premises at Stirling Street, off Manchester Road. The number of artists and portrait painters in Bradford after 1860 increased in response to the demands of ordinary people for a wider cultural perspective. Art, literature and music had, in pre-industrial times, retreated to the privacy of old established family houses and manorial halls. After 1850 this changed, and in cultural affairs the musical life of the town was improved when popular music became something more than the sacred music of church and chapel. The Gentleman's Glee Club had been formed in 1840 and in the same year a number of German residents established the Bradford Liedertafel. A number of Germans also helped Samuel Smith and Joshua Mann to found the Subscription Concert Committee in 1864. In the field of literature, Bradford had possessed a Library Society since 1774. A number of philosophical societies also emerged, albeit intermittently, to advance the townspeople's intellectual frontiers. Hostility and apathy prevented a permanent respectable theatre from being founded in Bradford until 1836, but the quality of Smedley's Peel Square Theatre in that year did much to improve the public's opinion of drama in Bradford, and by 1841, a fine stone building was erected as the Theatre Royal in Duke Street.

By 1850 there was some local demand for portrait and landscape painters as wealthier families sought to capture for posterity favourite views and faces. Sowden played a part in establishing the Bradford Artists' Society of Painting and Sculpture and mounting several exhibitions of paintings which were patronised by an increasing number of Bradford millowners and manufacturers. Sowden himself (from his diaries) painted for Edward Salt, Isaac Holden and Henry Mason. As Master of the Institute's School of Art, and later as founder and president of the Bradford Art Society, he was able to gather around him young men of considerable artistic talent, men like Ernest Sichel (1862-1941) who exhibited at the Royal Academy in 1885. Sowden himself had first exhibited there in 1863 with a water colour 'May blossom and nest'. Sowden's work was much influenced by William Hunt though he believed it possible to 'combine fidelity of detail with truth in broad effect'. His final Royal Academy showing in 1892, 'Whitby from Larpool' is a successful example of this theory.

Despite his success as a professional painter, Sowden never stinted from his work as a teacher at the Art School where he continued to take classes in the afternoon and evenings following a morning's work on business matters at the office. His diaries (1869-1923), kept at the West Yorkshire Archives Service in Bradford, reveal the wide variety of his interests, from painting and picture sales, and the teaching of art, to property development and commercial dealing.

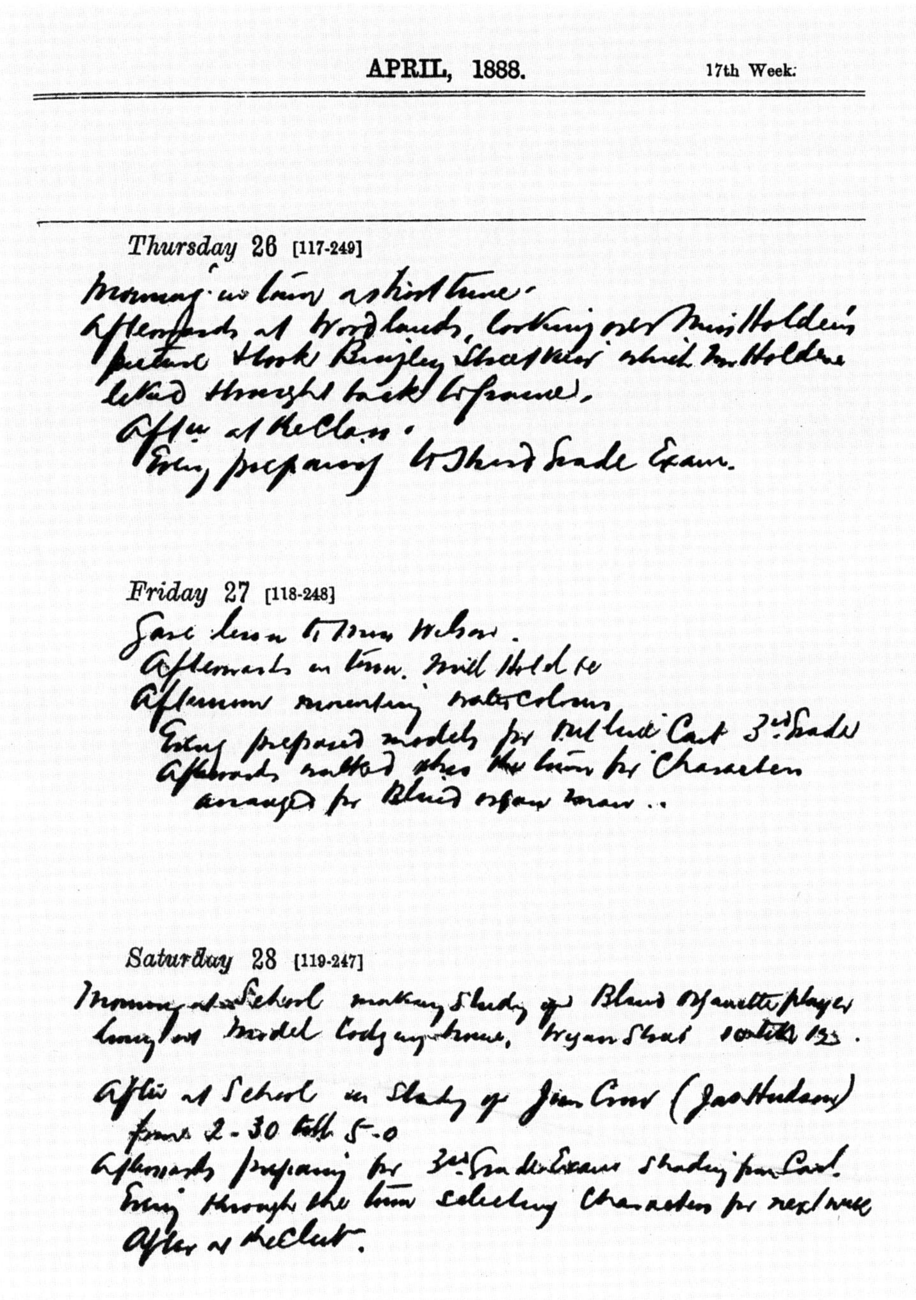
APRIL, 1888. 17th Week.

Thursday 26 [117-249]

Morning in town a short time.
Afterwards at Woodlands, looking over Miss Holden's pictures & took Bingley 'Shakspear' which Mr Holden lent & brought back to frame.
After at the Class.
Evening preparing to Third Grade Exam.

Friday 27 [118-248]

Gave lesson to Miss Wilson.
Afterwards in town. Mill Holdke
Afternoon mounting water colours
Evening prepared models for Outline Cast 3rd Grade
afterwards walked thro' the town for Characters
arranged for Blind organ man..

Saturday 28 [119-247]

Morning at School making Study of Blind organette player
[illegible] model lodging house. Wyan Street [illegible] till 1.30.
After at School on Study of Jim Crow (Jas Hudson)
from 2-30 till 5-0
Afterwards preparing for 3rd Grade Exam Shading from Cast.
Evening through the town selecting Characters for next week.
After at the Club.

Figure 1. A page from John Sowden's diary

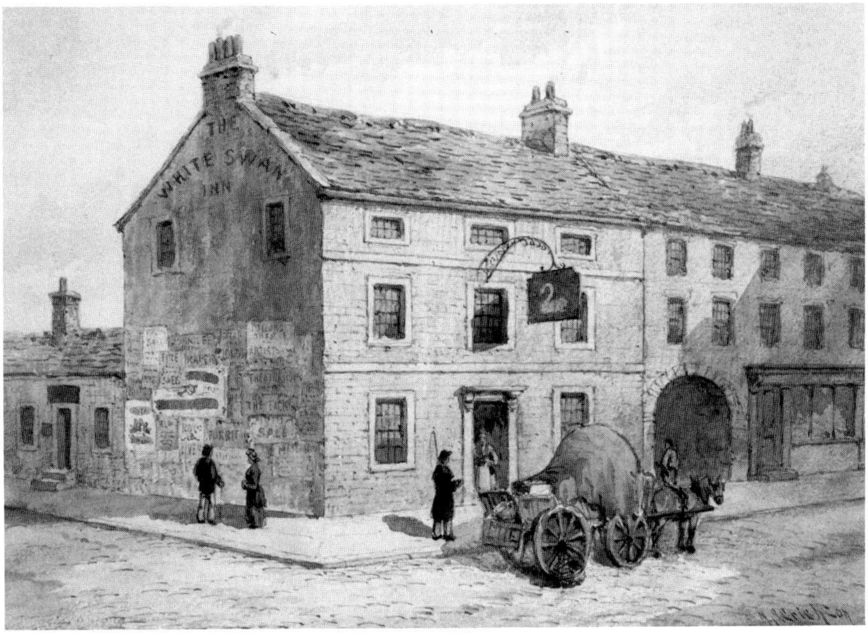

Figure 2. The White Swan Inn.
Painting by N.S. Crichton, early 1870s.

Sowden's architectural training, his eye for design and his upbringing in the building trade, all contributed to his talent for property development. Following his father's death in 1875, he inherited sufficient estates and capital to enable him to put that talent to profitable use. He purchased several inner city sites for mill and residential development. He also took advantage of the needs of the worsted trade for warehousing accommodation and he was an early speculator in the development of the Eastbrook estate (subsequently known as 'Little Germany'). Sowden's principal partner in these property deals was the well known Bradford clothier and tailor, George Brown. One of their most successful transactions was the purchase of The White Swan Inn (Fig. 2) and its resale for the development of a new concept in Victorian retailing, the shopping arcade. On the site between Market Street and Brook Street was erected the Swan Arcade (Fig. 3) an impressive structure of sixty-five market rooms and several

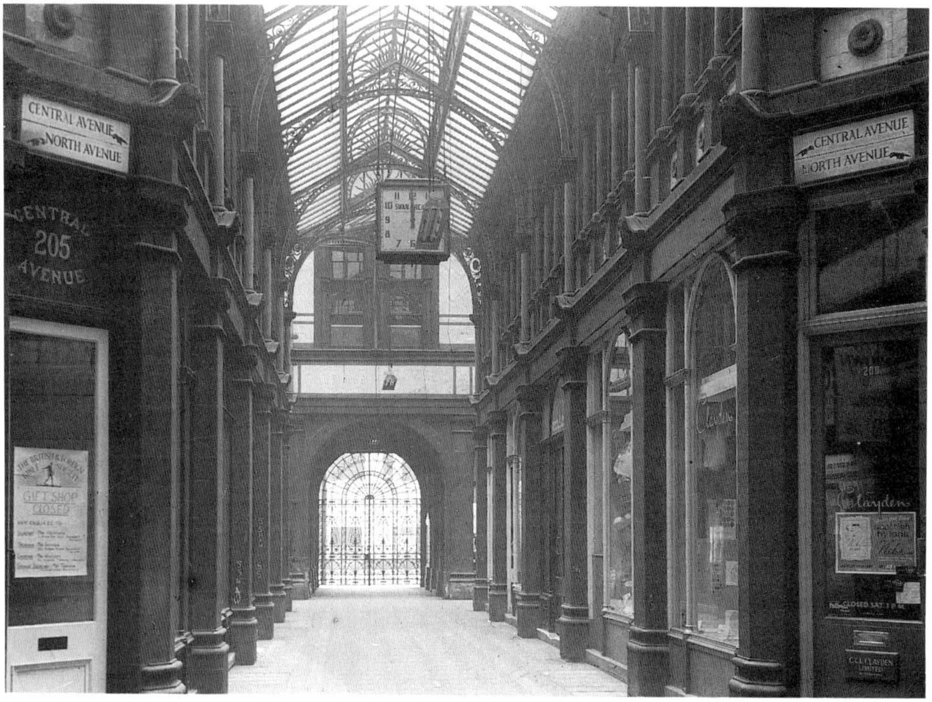

Figure 3. The Swan Arcade in 1961.

warehouses, in addition to the numerous shops and offices on the ground floor. Its ornate arcades and interior glasswork provided a home for several Bradford artists in later years.

During his early manhood, when he had something of a reputation as a 'Bohemian', Sowden travelled extensively across the Continent and into Northern Europe. At the age of 48 in 1886 he settled down and married Anne Bowes, the fourth daughter of a Bradford solicitor. Sowden took his new bride into his recently acquired home at 1, Blenheim Road (Fig. 4), a large end terraced property in the fashionable middle-class suburb of Manningham, where he constructed an artists' studio in the top storey of the building.

In the following year Anne Sowden gave birth to her one and only child, a son, John Russell, and thereafter she seems to have spent most of her time with her young son, or confined to her

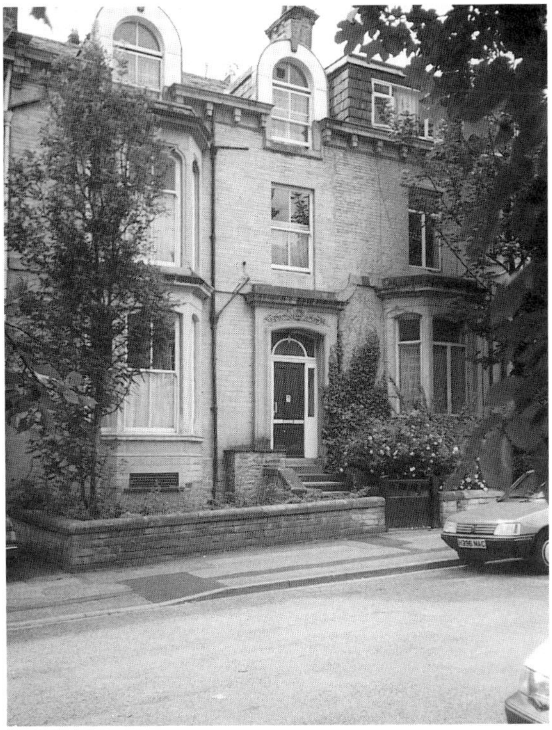

Figure 4. 1, Blenheim Road today.

bedroom with one illness or another. Sowden threw himself into his work and his art. His endless round of business, teaching and painting was only broken by generous holidays in North Wales, the Lake District and abroad, or by weekends away in Morecambe, Whitby and the Yorkshire Dales. For many years he was president of the Bradford Art Society and between 1904-06 was Vice President of the Yorkshire Union of Artists. He exhibited at the Royal Academy in 1888, 1890 and 1892. Later he became a Committee member of the Bradford Historical and Antiquarian Society and a vice-president of the Bradford Scientific Society. He was a director of the Mechanics' Institute, the East Morley Savings Bank, and of the Bradford Third Equitable Building Society. In his private life Sowden seems to have found immense joy at being with his son. Albeit a sickly child, John Russell went with his father on numerous painting trips both at home and abroad. Both became keen gardeners and botanists. As Mrs Sowden became more and more of a recluse, father and son enjoyed winter skating on Keighley Tarn and summer botany trips to Beckfoot and Bolton Abbey. By the mid-1890s, Anne Sowden was described by her husband as 'rather melancholy'. Apart from Sunday walks around Manningham Park with her husband and son, she appears to have withdrawn almost entirely from public life. Illness or the Victorian code of respectability seems to have tied her to the family home and a circumscribed social life with relatives and close family friends. Like many other Victorian gentlemen, her husband, who was much older than his wife, sought male company 'in the club'. In John Sowden's case it was the Bradford Liberal Club in Bank Street where he could be found every Saturday night with a regular party of billiard players, distinctly dressed with fastidious care and invariably with a flower in his buttonhole and a cigar in his hand. He was a committee member of the Liberal Club for thirty years and chairman on several occasions. He canvassed for the party at election times and attended at the Liberal Club almost to the end of his life.

His unexciting home life and his routine commercial world were stimulated however by his painting. His holidays were devoted almost entirely to his art; his paints and easel went with him to Belgium, France, Denmark, Greece and the Tyrol. For all his travelling it was Bradford, his home town, which was the source of his greatest creative genius – his gallery of portraits of notable citizens and local street characters.

Between 1887 and 1901, when he retired from his position as headmaster of the Mechanics' Institute Art School, Sowden painted dozens of characters from the streets of Bradford. With increasing uniformity of dress, speech and manners, and the manipulations of mass culture and society, the quirks and eccentricities of these Bradford characters were under threat. In October 1893 his diary reveals that he purchased in Baildon, a copy of Henry Mayhew's 'London Labour and London Poor'. Mayhew had estimated that only about a third of the labouring people in England and Wales were fully employed; another third were partially employed, and the remaining third were wholly unemployed at any given time. Owing to the large numbers of people on the labour market Mayhew concluded that many jobs were not full time jobs at all but casual labour influenced by the vagaries of the market, the seasonal weather, and the physical ability of the worker to withstand sickness or old age. Equally there were those who did not want regular work, those who genuinely preferred an itinerant life, particularly in the warm weather of the summer months when they found farm work in the countryside, only to return in winter to take up street trading and hawking.

It was this category of the labouring poor that Sowden portrayed in his paintings. Below them were the vagrant and the criminal class. Sowden seems to have had nothing to do with these 'rough' and disreputable elements of the lower classes, his paintings are only of those 'respectable' casual labourers who moved uneasily, sometimes precariously, on the interface between irregular work and full employment – the crippled factory worker, the disabled soldier, the immigrant Irish and itinerant Italian, what Henry Mayhew called the 'wandering tribes'. Sowden's purchase of Mayhew's book is indicative of one talent recognising another. Both men, using different media, were concerned with those shadowy 'comers and goers' on the periphery of Victorian city life. Their pedlars, hawkers and itinerants were the 'real' men and women of mid-nineteenth century town life. Sowden's portraits are as important as registers of popular taste, fashion and cultural attitudes as are the biographical sketches of Henry Mayhew. Both provide a vivid and realistic social record of the lower classes of their time. Today the daily life of the Victorian city seems remote and possibly irrecoverable, but John Sowden, by courtesy of the Bradford Arts, Museums and Libraries Division, has left us another rich and colourful source for understanding Victorian culture and society in his fascinating gallery of portraits of Bradford characters and worthies from the last quarter of the nineteenth century.

THE CHARACTERS

John Sowden said in a lecture to the Bradford Antiquarian Society in 1908:

> *Not the least interesting feature of every age is that group of people who by their oddities and eccentric behaviour attain to some measure of local fame.*
> *These psychological freaks present to the investigator of the workings of the human mind, past or present, much interesting material and there is a picturesque element about their vagaries of action and dress that has always appealed to the artist.*

The idea for this remarkable and unique collection has its origins in the art class at the Mechanics' Institute in the mid-1880s. Professor Hercomer had painted several portraits of street characters to prove to art students the potential for good art amid even the most prosaic surroundings of everyday life. To convince his students Sowden proceeded to paint in water colour, a handful of Bradford's leading 'comers and goers'. Inspired and enthused by his own success others were added to his gallery until fifty-eight characters were placed on permanent record alongside two hundred and fifty prominent 'worthies' of Victorian Bradford. Notwithstanding the quality of the latter it is the street vendors, pedlars, hawkers and eccentrics of a typical Victorian city which catch the eye and fire the imagination. Sowden's diaries for the 1880s are littered with studio appointments, chance meetings and street encounters with the flotsam and jetsam of Bradford's city life.

1888 seems to have been a prolific year for Sowden's characters as his diary shows no less than forty-six of Bradford's street people visiting his studio including Dick Delaney, Fish David, Mary Ann Byrom, John Claverie, George Pinchin, John Ross and the crippled fiddle player James Mannis.

Sowden later wrote:

> *For many years I have been in touch with the men and women who parade our streets as mendicants and hawkers and who certainly form a most picturesque element in our everyday life.*

His gallery of characters was publicly exhibited along with his other works in 1891 and again in 1897 and 1906. Five years before his death, Sowden offered the whole collection of 315 portraits to the Corporation of Bradford. Thanks to Sowden's keen eye for observation of individual detail, such characters as Pot Mary, Whistling Tom, Fish David and Dick Delaney can be as well known to Bradfordians of today as they were to those who walked the streets of Bradford a hundred years ago. The old artist, who died at his Manningham home in January 1926, had left for future generations of Bradfordians an accurate and colourful reminder of their late Victorian forebears.

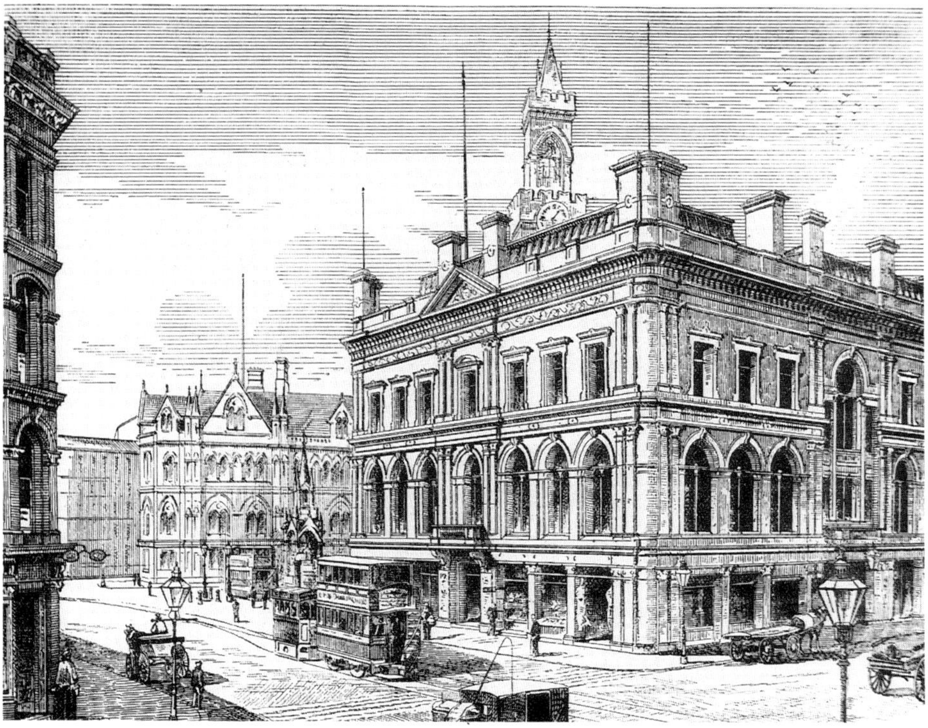

Figure 5. The Mechanics' Institute, Bradford, 1888.

THE CHARACTERS: THE PAINTINGS OF JOHN SOWDEN

1. Dick DELANEY

Dick Delaney was one of thousands of Irishmen who left their native land in the 1840s to find work and homes in the industrial cities of northern England. Many slipped into the ranks of the unemployed or criminal classes but Delaney managed to keep his head above water for several years, first as a weaver at Rand's Mill, and later as a publican. His lost licence may have had something to do with the fact that he supplied two qualities of beer from the same barrel. Later, with a donkey and cart, he became one of hundreds of Bradford's costermongers, earning an honest living by hawking. The costers make up a large category of Sowden's colourful street characters. They had an important part to play in retailing history, in that transitionary stage from markets to shop retailing. By their speech and dress they were a coherent community set apart from most other Bradfordians. Destitute men and widowed mothers turned to street trading for a living with its limited capital investment and precariously small turnover. They were abused by the public, hounded by policemen and shopocracy, and exposed to the ravages of the English climate. Little wonder they were a resilient, cheeky and aggressive lot. Dick Delaney, born in Connaught in 1827, was perhaps the best known of Bradford's street hawkers and was certainly a favourite of the artist. His natural wit and readiness to see the funny side of life made him popular with adults, and his horse and cart, harnessed together by a miscellaneous assortment of ropes, rags and strings, made him a general favourite with young children.

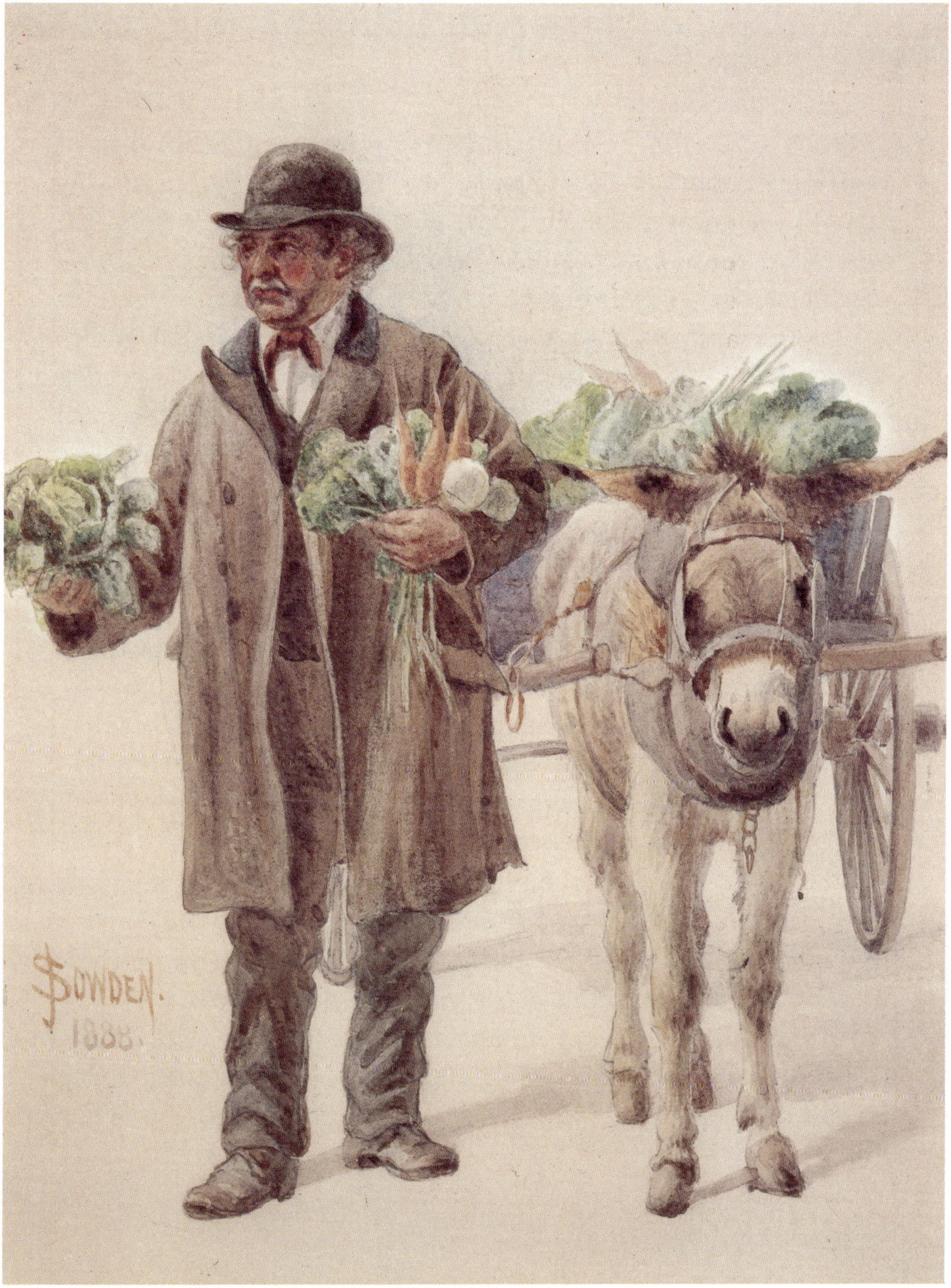

S BOWDEN.
1888.

2. Mary Ann BYROM

Delaney with his donkey and cart was one of the elite of Bradford's costers as the majority like Mary Ann Byrom usually hawked their wares (wood, celery, vegetables) from baskets. She was better known as 'Apple Mary', aged 63, selling fruit and vegetables not far from the Green Market behind Christ Church. She had formerly worked in service and lived in the White Abbey district and came into town each day on the wagonette service between Ivegate and Whetley Hill. As she grew older her enormous frame meant that she could only travel from home into town on one particular wagon which had a doorway large enough to admit her. Consequently she gave up her 'patch' in the town centre and sold her wares in Manningham. Sowden's diary notes (14th November 1888).

> *I arranged for this particular bus on a certain day which would land her in Godwin Street. I waited a long time for her and at last I thought I would go to the stand and see what had become of her. I found her out on a doorstep puffing away like a steam engine. With a little more patience I got her down to my town studio with the result you see.*

What a sight they must have been! The respectable man-about-town escorting the fat and somewhat disreputable old hawker through the main streets of Bradford in broad daylight. Sowden was obviously no respecter of the Victorian class system.

As was customary for all female hawkers, *Apple Mary* always wore a white apron. Clothes like this were coarse and made to last for several years.

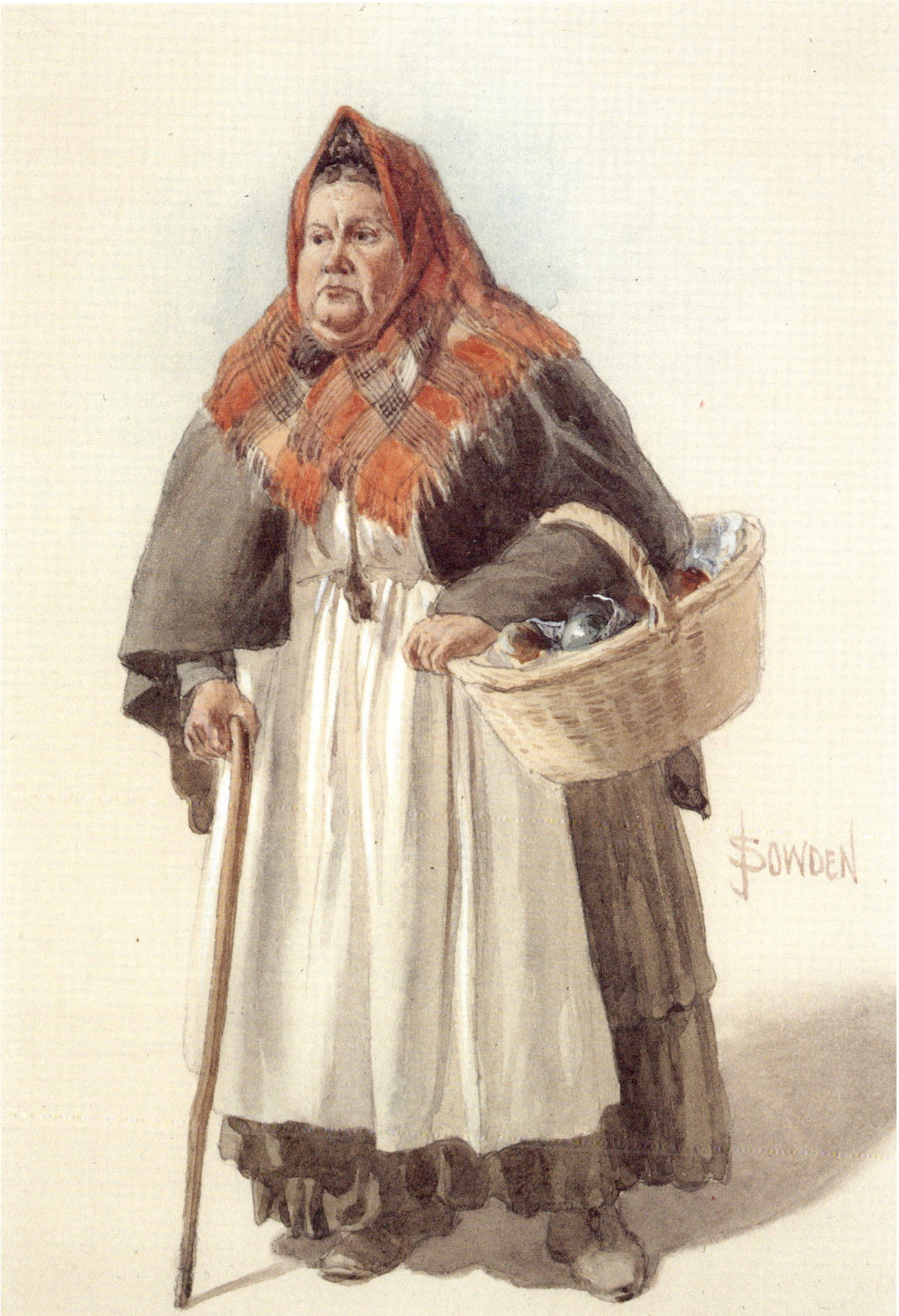
SOWDEN

3. Eliza SUNTER

Another familiar lady coster to Bradford's streets was Eliza Sunter, otherwise known as *Old Betty.* When she sat for Sowden on Wednesday, 4 July 1888, she was 68 years old and had been hawking tapes, buttons and needles for thirty years, with her blind and infirm husband. She was born in Grassington in 1820 and was always well respected by her neighbours and hawking peers. After the death of her husband she maintained and cared for another aged and crippled female coster. Both of them lived on 2/6 (12½p) a week from the parish, in dingy premises on Bolton Road behind the Duke of Devonshire inn.

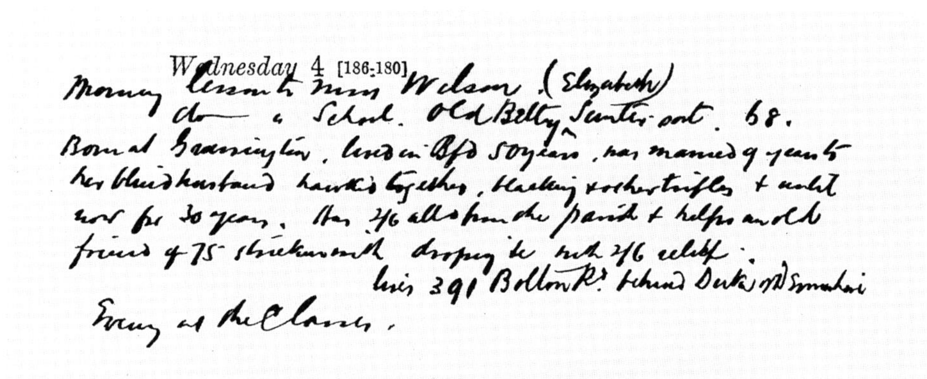

Wednesday 4 [186-180]
Morning Lesson to Miss Wilson (Elizabeth)
do a School. Old Betty Sunter - sat. 68.
Born at Grassington, lived in Bfd 50 years, was married 9 years to
her blind husband hawking together, [illegible] & other trifles + [illegible]
now for 30 years. Has 2/6 allow from the parish + helps an old
friend of 75 [illegible] dropping [illegible] 2/6 relief.
lives 391 Bolton Rd. behind Duke of Devonshire
Evening at the Classes.

John Sowden's diary. Wednesday 4th July, 1888.

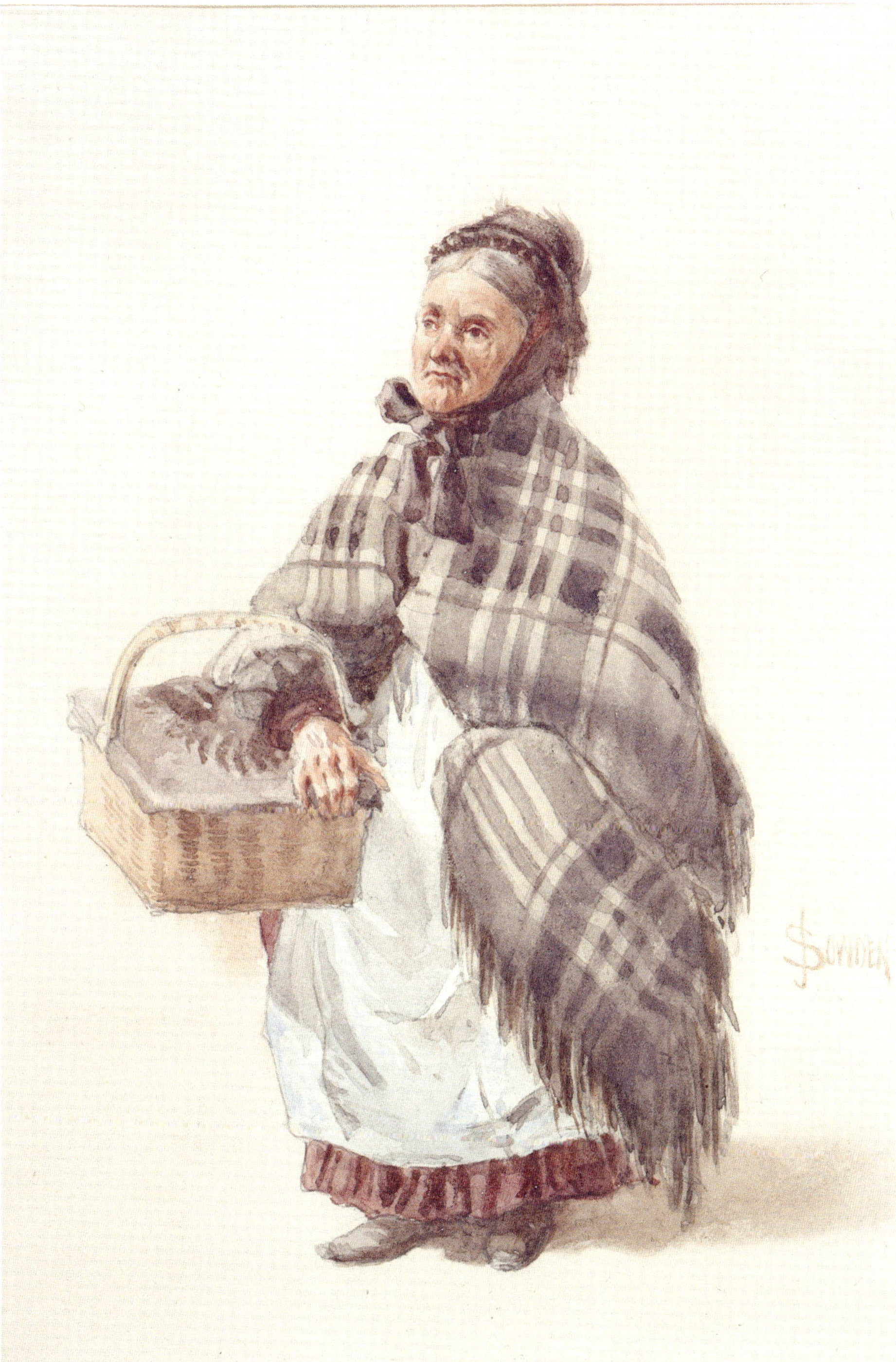

4. Bridget CROWN

Bridget followed *Old Betty* Sunter into the studio of John Sowden in July 1888. She was born on the Emerald Isle in 1820 and for over forty years had hawked small wares in Ivegate. With her bright brown skirt, light green shawl, white apron and distinctive red headscarf, she cut a colourful figure in the dingy yards and alleyways behind the Sun Inn. She is described by Sowden as a hawker of nettles and pots. For those on the poverty line nettle soup might mean the difference between hunger and starvation.

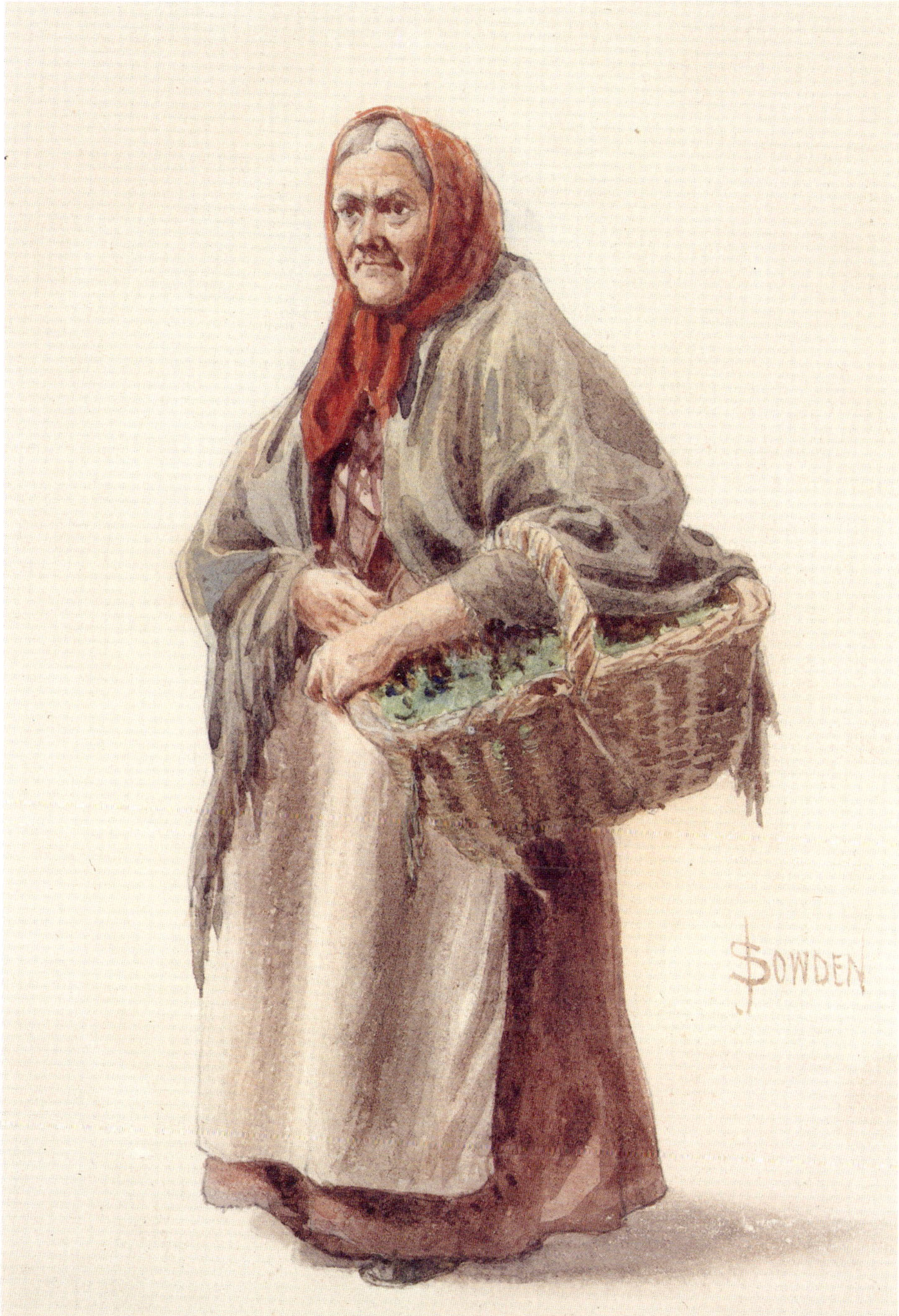
SOWDEN

5. James MANNIS

In these days of the Welfare State, society's unfortunates are cushioned from the hardships of unemployment, disability and old age, but the Victorian Poor Law provided only a crutch by which a stricken individual might haul himself up. James Mannis was 54 when he sat for Sowden on Friday 25 May 1888. Since the age of 13 he had been crippled from the waist. He wheeled himself about the town in a three-wheeled contraption made for him by his friends. He played the violin and begged from passers-by. His bitterness and bad language made him a disagreeable character and he was constantly being asked to 'move on' and out of the town. Sowden noted in his diary that Mannis had 'visited all the principal towns and cities in England'.

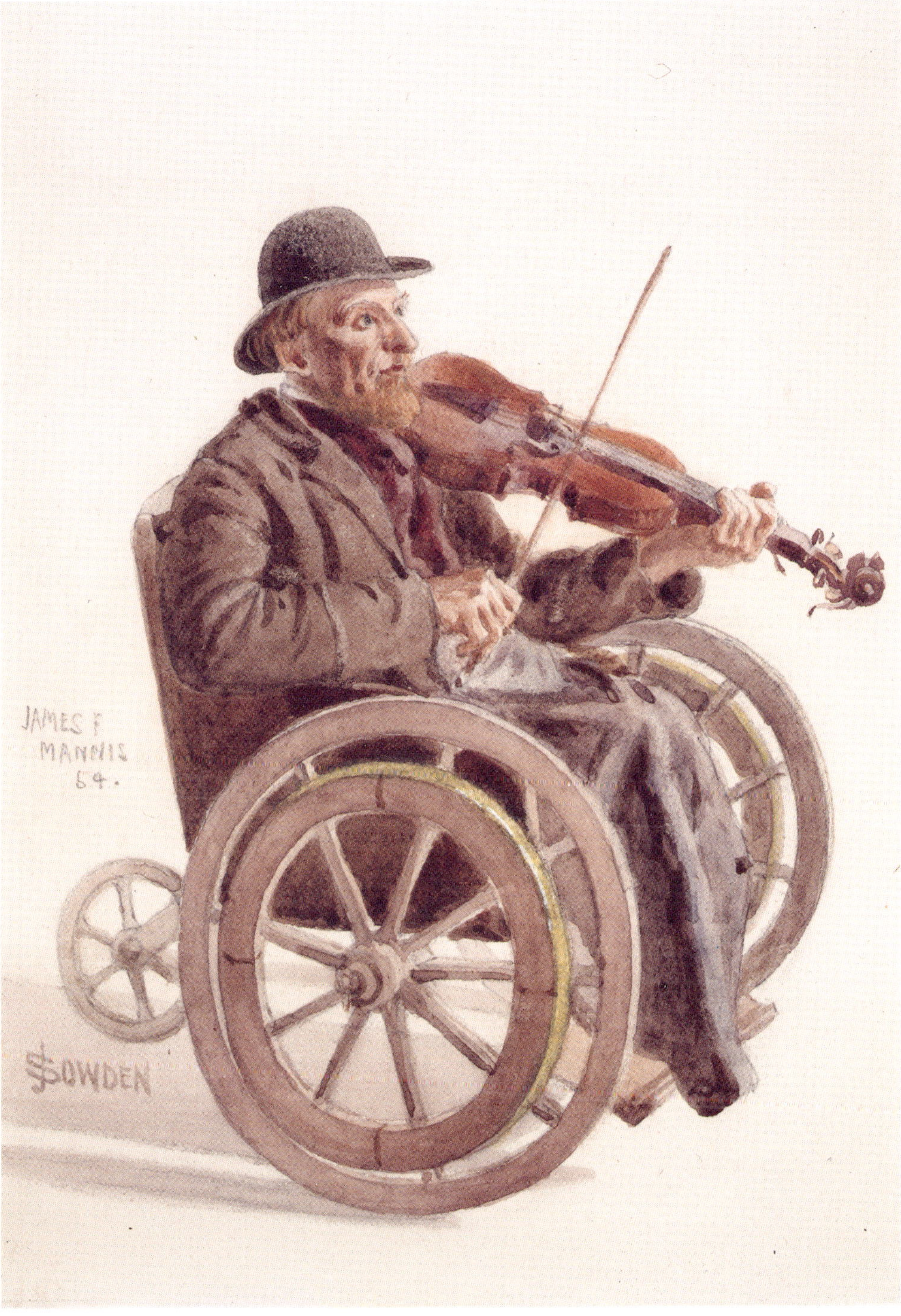
JAMES F
MANNIS
54.
SOWDEN

6. Ellen HARGREAVES

Another infirm street musician was Ellen Hargreaves, a blind concertina player, whose pitch was usually in front of the Midland Station accompanied by a little girl or boy as her guide. Ellen sat for Sowden on May Day 1888 at the studio in the Mechanics' Institute. When the sitting was finished Ellen's guide had disappeared. Before the arrival of James Ashley (Salt Jim) Sowden volunteered to accompany the blind woman back to the Midland Station. On the way along Market Street he gave Ellen his arm to guide her. Passing the Exchange they passed several prominent businessmen known to Sowden. They were disgusted that the elegant city gent in frock coat and spats should conduct a known beggar in broad daylight. The Victorian cult of respectability had been broken by Sowden. The rough and the respectable just did not come together in this way.

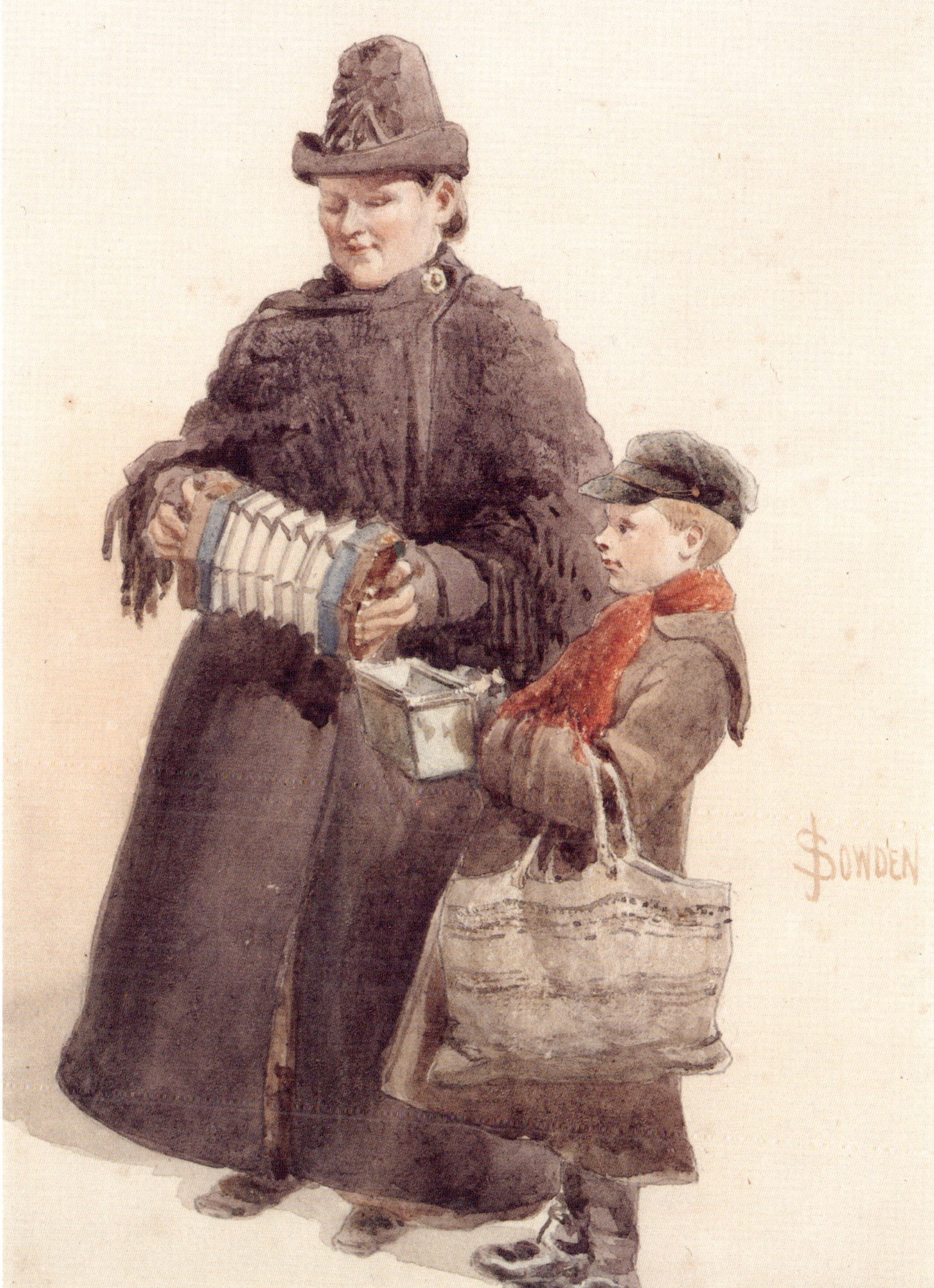
BOWDEN

7. James ASHLEY

James Ashley, more commonly known as *Salt Jim,* spent his days wandering the main streets of Bradford in search of a buyer for the bar of salt which he supposedly carried beneath his shabby coat. This was only a pretext for his begging activities which served him well, for, on being arrested for begging he was taken to the Town Hall, searched, and was found to possess fifteen shillings. Ashley visited Sowden's town centre studio on the afternoon of the first day of May in 1888.

Salt Jim died in the old Bradford Workhouse in Little Horton Lane where the doctor certified him as 'half witted', but there were plenty in Bradford during Jim's lifetime who were in full possession of their senses, and who fared nothing like as well as Jim. When he died he had over £200 in an account at the Bradford Bank, a fact he made known during his life when he admitted to begging because all his money was in the bank!

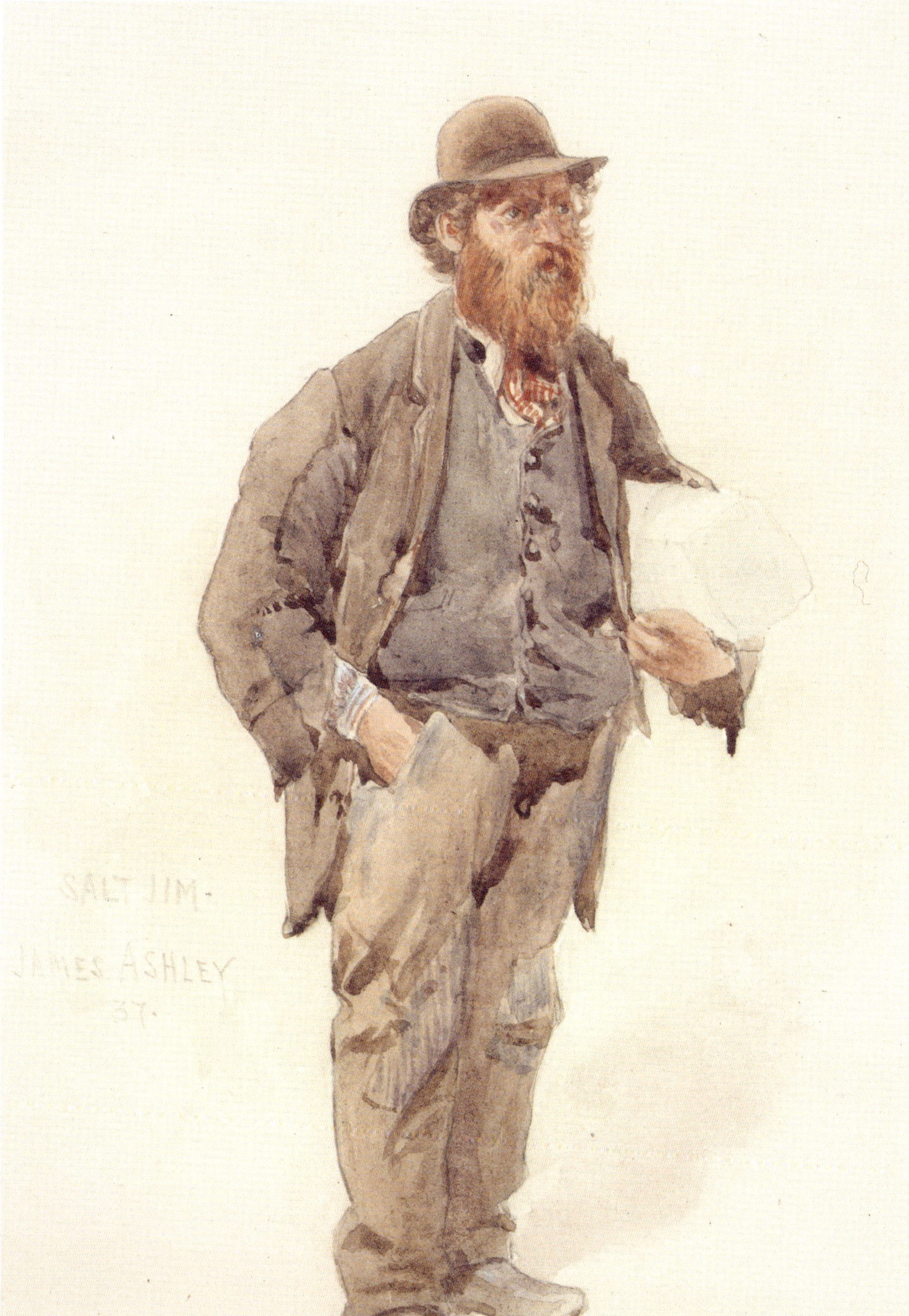
SALT JIM -
JAMES ASHLEY
87.

8. George MURPHY

George Murphy was better known as *Old Clo* from his hawking 'call' as a dealer in cast-off clothing. It is said he had formerly been in service as a gentleman's valet and, as such, kept his respectability by always wearing top hat and frock coat. Murphy was born in Queens County, Ireland in 1827 but came to Bradford at the age of 23 like thousands of other Irishmen and women at that time. Before entering service he worked as a tailor. When Sowden painted him in November, 1890, Murphy had been selling second hand clothes for 30 years in his distinctive businessman's costume.

Sowden's diary for 18th November 1890 says:

> *Expected George Murphy at 10 o'clock but had to go fetch him at 11.30 and at 12 o'clock he turned up and I painted until nearly 2.00. Had dinner at the club and painted from 2.45 till nearly 4 and finished.*

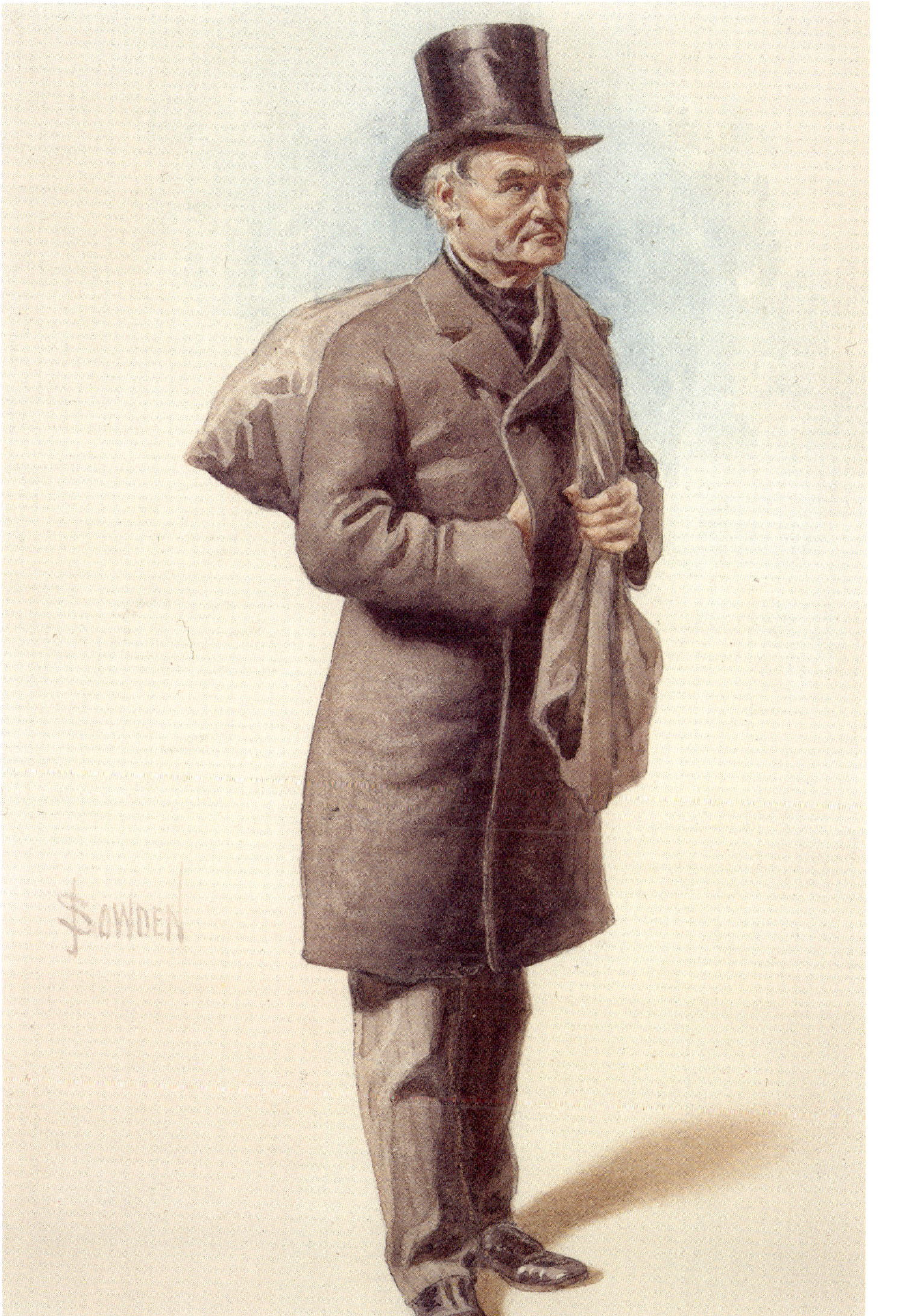
BOWDEN

9. Abraham JOHNSON

Abraham Johnson was one of half a dozen black men in Victorian Bradford. He was 40 years old and was a native of Zanzibar where he was enslaved as a teenager. His slavery took him to China, Japan and India where he escaped and worked his passage to England. He found work at John Marshall's flax mill in Leeds. He was married with a baby daughter and lived in a common lodging house in Bradford. At the time of his portrait Johnson sold penny tracts and broadsheets round the town. Sowden had spent some months locating Johnson's whereabouts and was relieved and pleased to have 'secured' his sitting in June 1888.

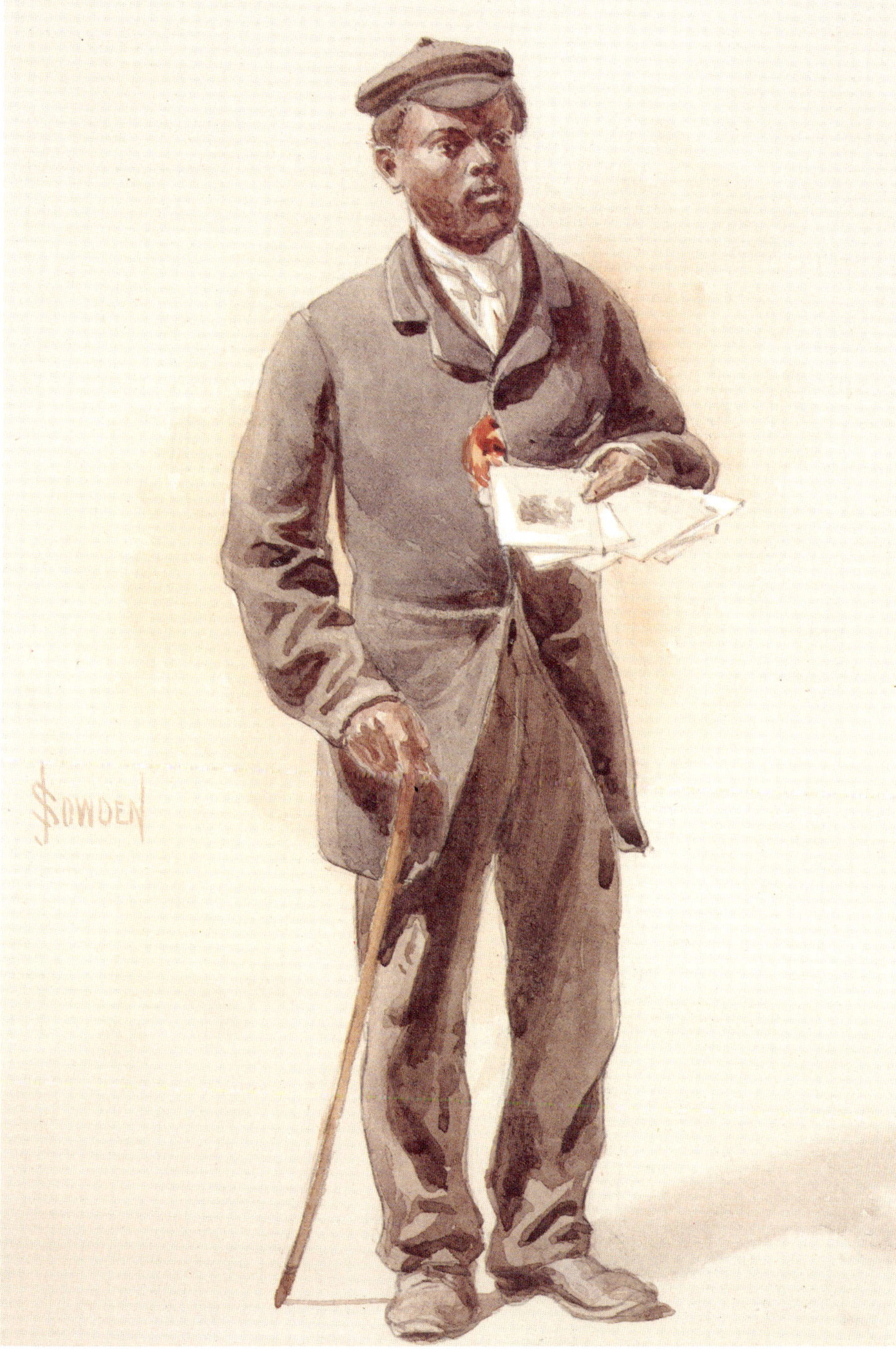
SOWDEN

10. John CLAVERIE

John Claverie (*Monsieur*) was an aged Frenchman (78) who had formerly worked in a bookmakers. But he lived chiefly on the money gained from selling pens and pencils, as well as the money begged from respectable professional offices of architects, lawyers, etc., on the pretext of wanting to get sufficient money to get back to France. He never got enough for he died shortly afterwards in a common lodging house – the night time haven of the wandering tribes. In Victorian times most towns had streets given over entirely to lodging houses, condemned by reformers after 1850 for their promiscuity and their overcrowded and haphazard sleeping arrangements. But to a homeless wanderer like Claverie, without any family, the lodging house offered warmth, shelter and some companionship. Claverie posed for Sowden at the Mechanics' Institute studio in August 1888.

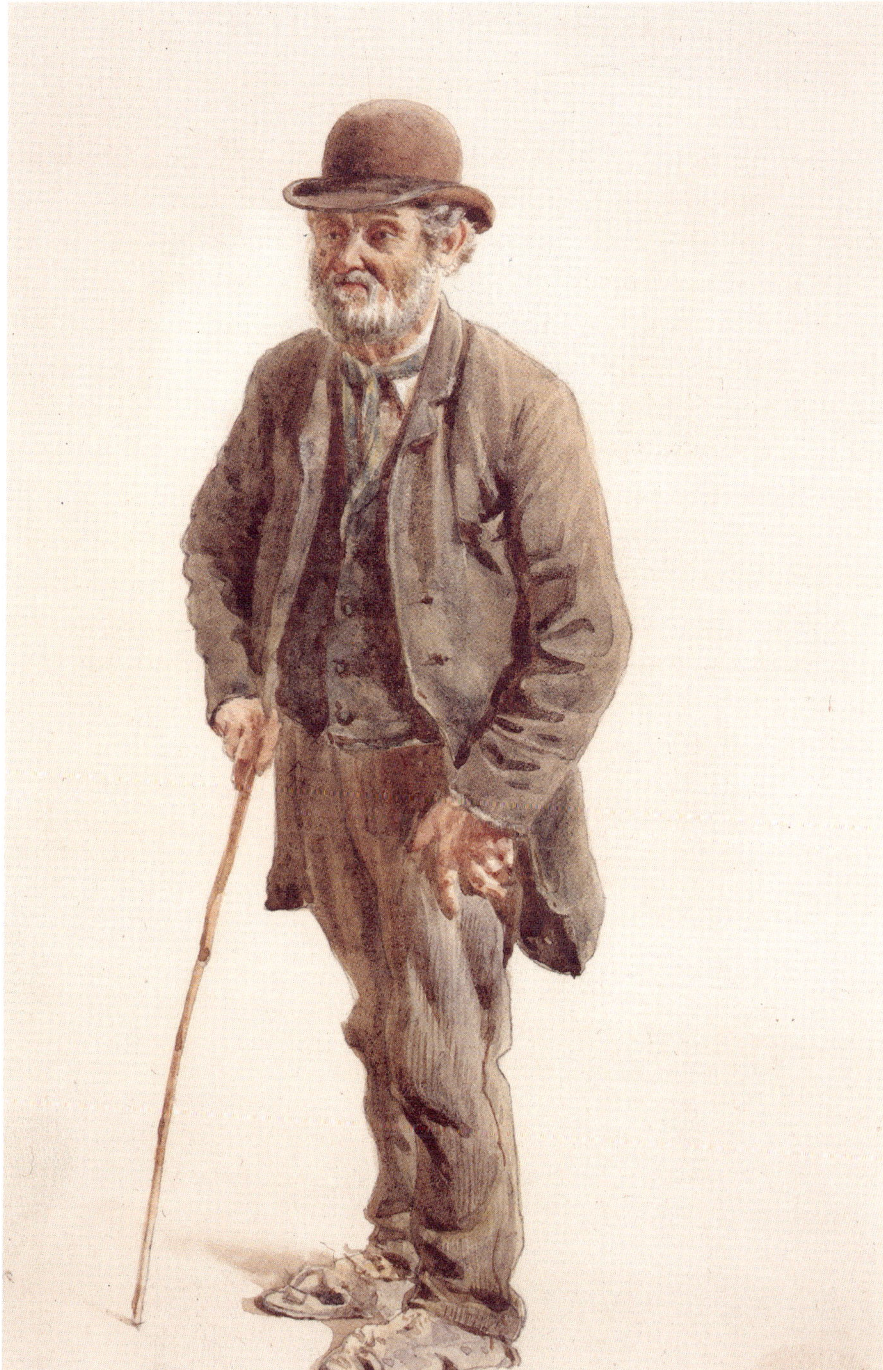

11. James FLETCHER

Blind Jim, christened Jem Fletcher, was 83 years of age when Sowden painted him. Born in Leeds, he came to Bradford in 1825, and for many years had patrolled the streets of the town as one of the original Christmas Waits, a group of itinerant musicians who played in the streets into the late hours of the night in the weeks before Christmas. The musicians, two violinists and a clarinet player, were all blind and linked together by means of a large pole held by a guide and leader who knew the route. Fletcher and Sam Smith were the fiddle players. In 1862 the Old Waits were superseded by a new band but only after a bitter public wrangle. Since that time Fletcher had played solo in Bradford's streets and public houses. He sat for Sowden on Friday 20th July between 2.30 and 6.00 in the afternoon. Fletcher had married a blind woman when he came to Bradford and their marriage lasted 43 years until her death, when he married again.

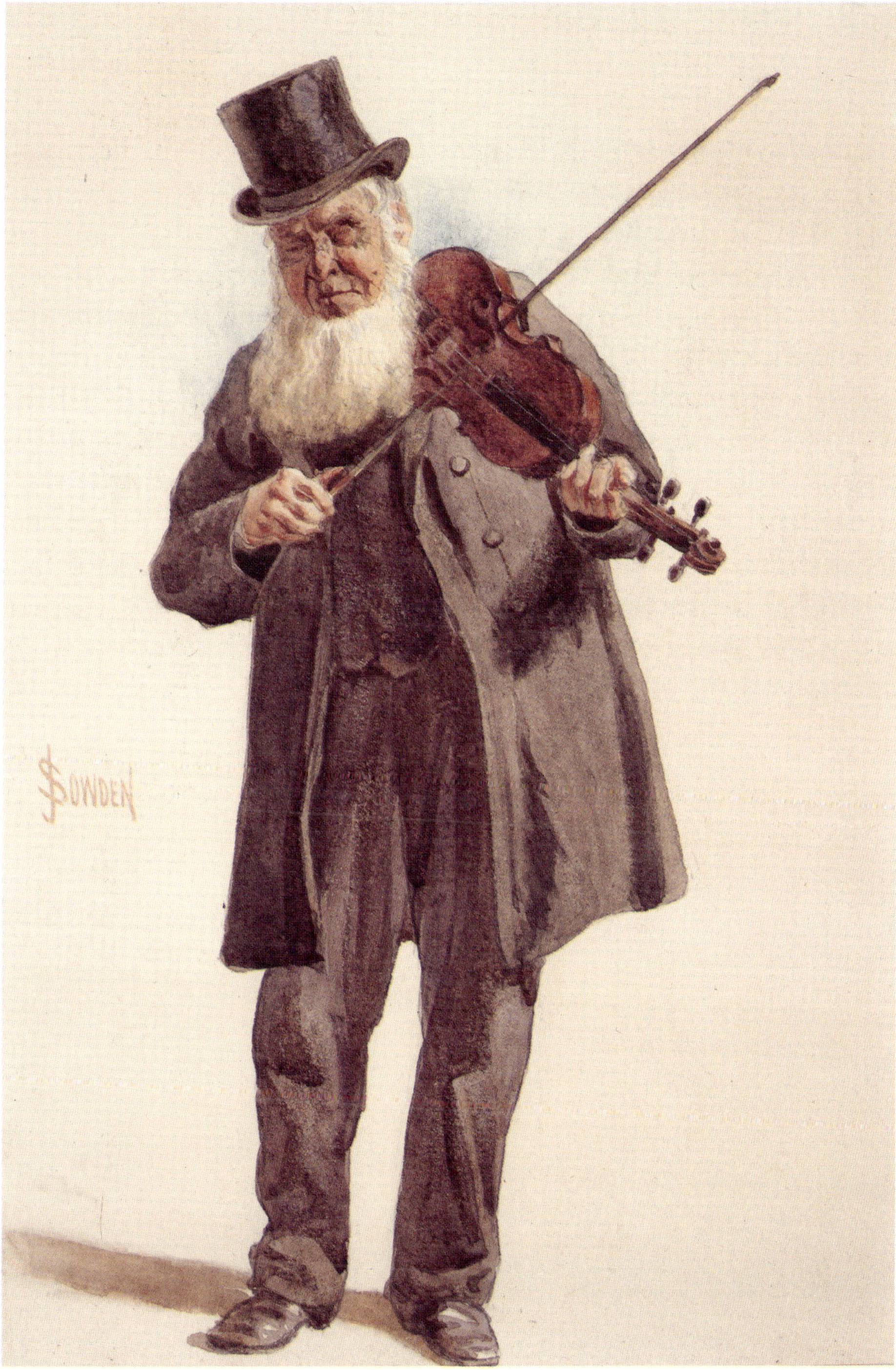
DOWDEN

12. Benjamin BOYES

Another well known street character was newsvendor Benjamin Boyes, renowned for his loud and deep barking voice when selling papers in the days before radio and television news bulletins. The *Bradford Observer* and *Leeds Mercury* were issued several times a day and Boyes' working day was a long one, long enough for him to make a change of clothing, for he wore a different costume in the evening from the one he had set out in first thing in the morning (hence Sowden's two separate portraits). On Sundays and Bank Holidays he was a familiar figure in the holiday crowds at the foot of Shipley Glen, selling his almanacs and pamphlets, making an extra shilling or two. In his diary Sowden notes that Boyes had been selling papers in Bradford since 1831 and that "he is the only man in the Bradford district to have sold unstamped* newspapers and almanacs".

* Until 1855 the government imposed a Stamp Duty on all newspapers. Each paper had a duty mark stamped on it.

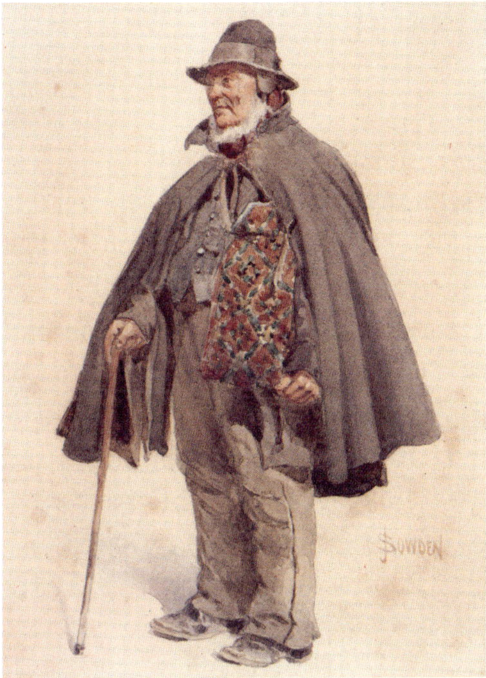
SOWDEN

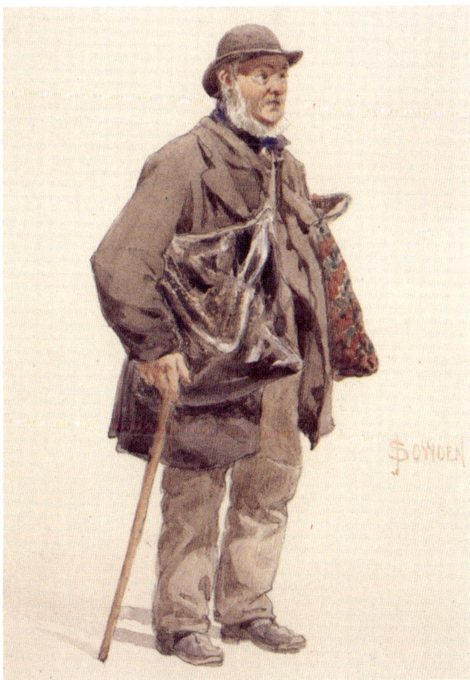
SOWDEN

13. Edward HOLMES

Edward Holmes sat twice for Sowden in early March, 1891. He was just 27 years old and after an apprenticeship had started his own business as a cabinet maker. Like other young men of his age he had been caught up in the new leisured society of the late Victorian period. In 1883 he had joined the Manningham Football Club as a forward in a sport which resembled rugby but which, like other sports, was becoming increasingly commercialised and competitive. He was made captain of the club in 1888 and in the year of his painting he was selected to play for the Yorkshire County Club. Here he sports the colours of the Manningham Club which played at what is now Valley Parade, home of Bradford City Football Club.

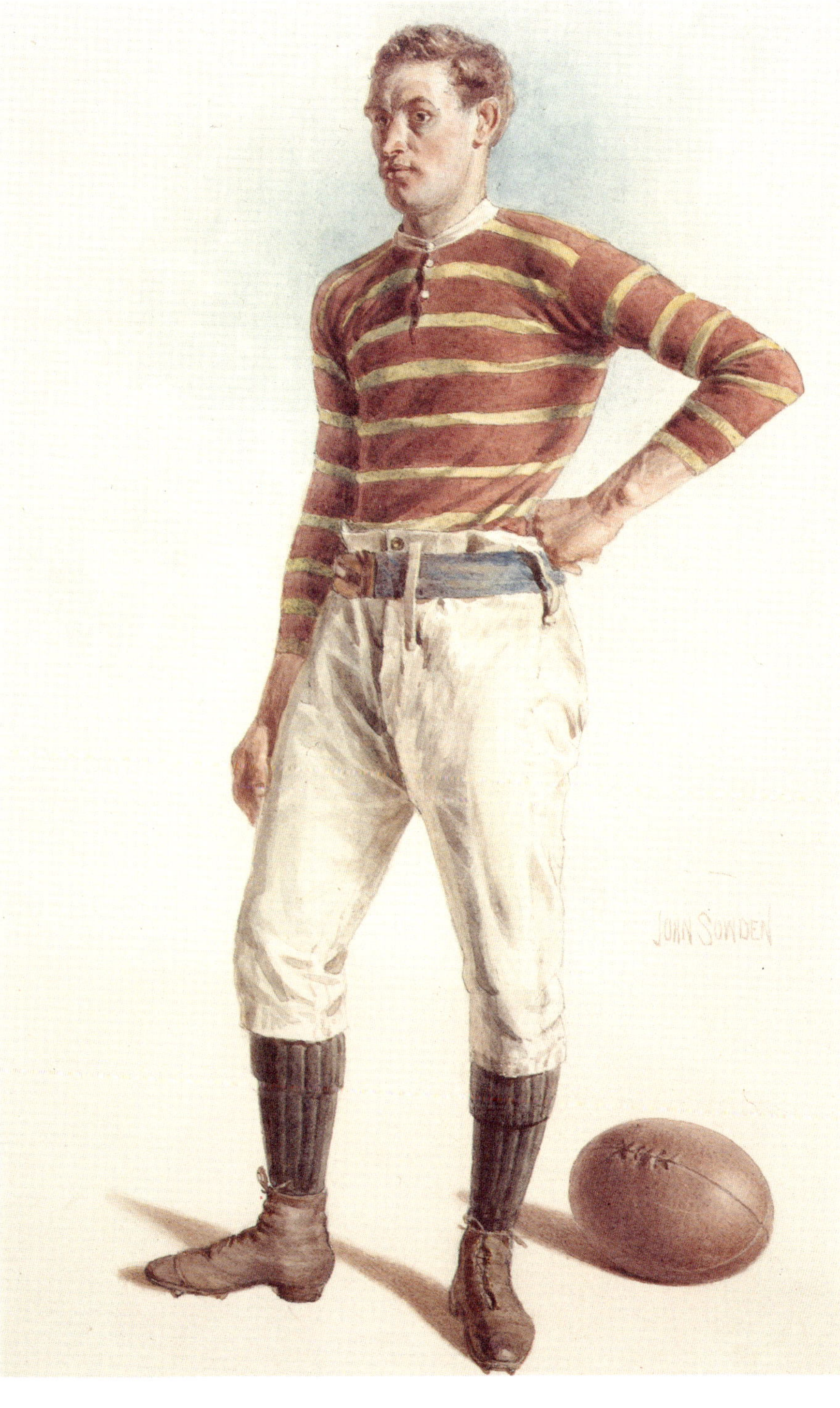
JOHN SOWDEN

14. Jabez HORNER

Mr Horner was born at Pateley Bridge in 1826 and came to Bradford with his widowed mother in 1835. From a fruit stall near Cuckoo Bridge (Hall Ings) he assisted his uncle, eventually taking his trade to the streets where he became one of the most influential of Bradford's fruit dealers. It was he who provided the fruit for the banquet at the opening of the Bradford Technical College on the visit of the Prince and Princess of Wales in 1887.

He was a good platform and stump orator on temperance matters and a teetotaller for almost thirty years. Horner arrived late for his portrait painting in July 1890 but eventually sat for two hours and a further two hours a week later.

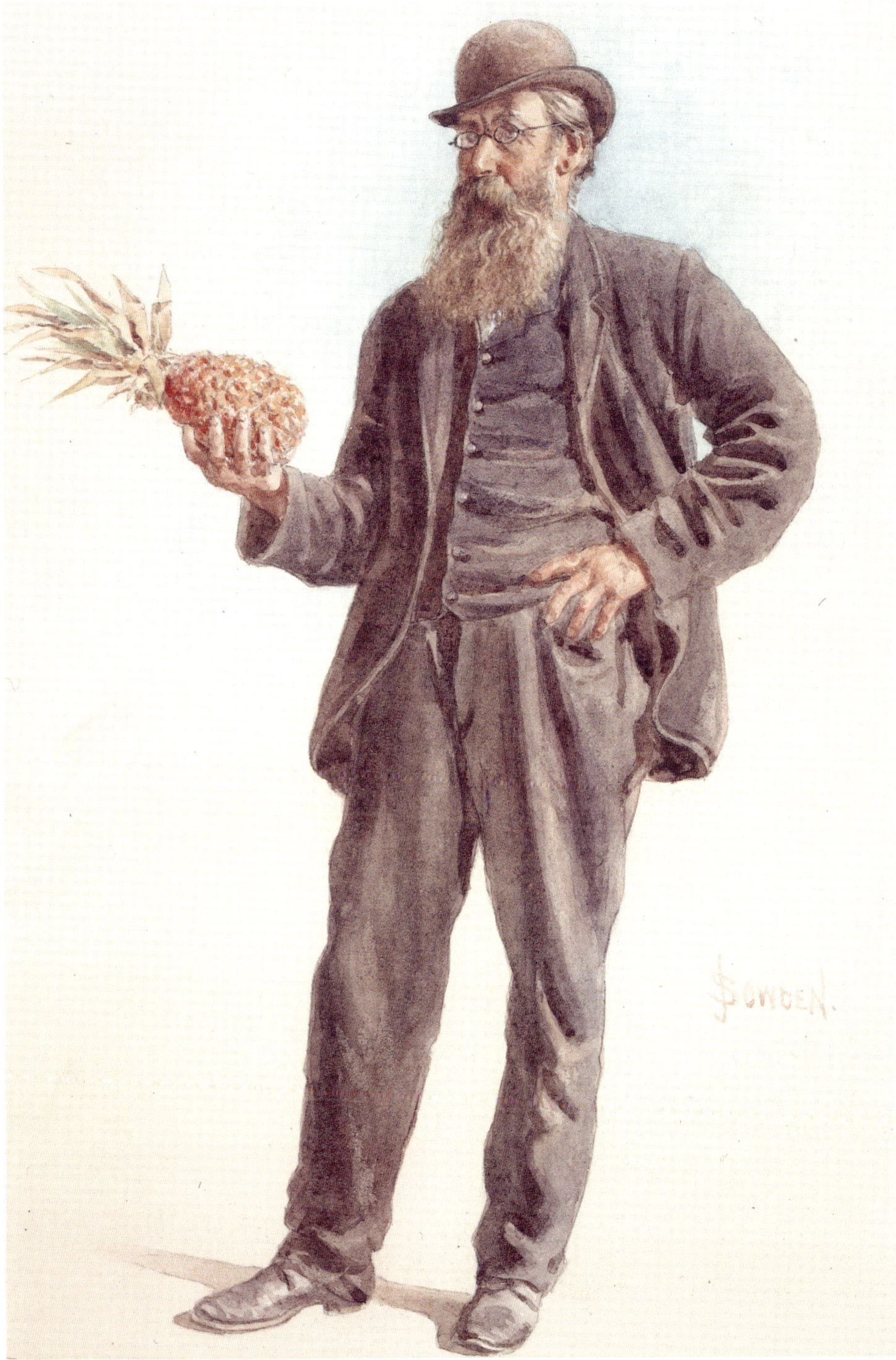

15. David VAUGHAN

More familiar to Bradfordians as *Fish David,* David Vaughan was a noted street hawker of game and fish. He frequented the Manchester Road area of Bradford having obtained his wares from the Fish market in Hammerton Street at 5 o'clock each morning. He was known to bring consternation to regular customers by calling out that fish he was selling today was not like the stinking fish of yesterday but had come fresh from the sea! David Vaughan sat for Sowden on 16th November 1888.

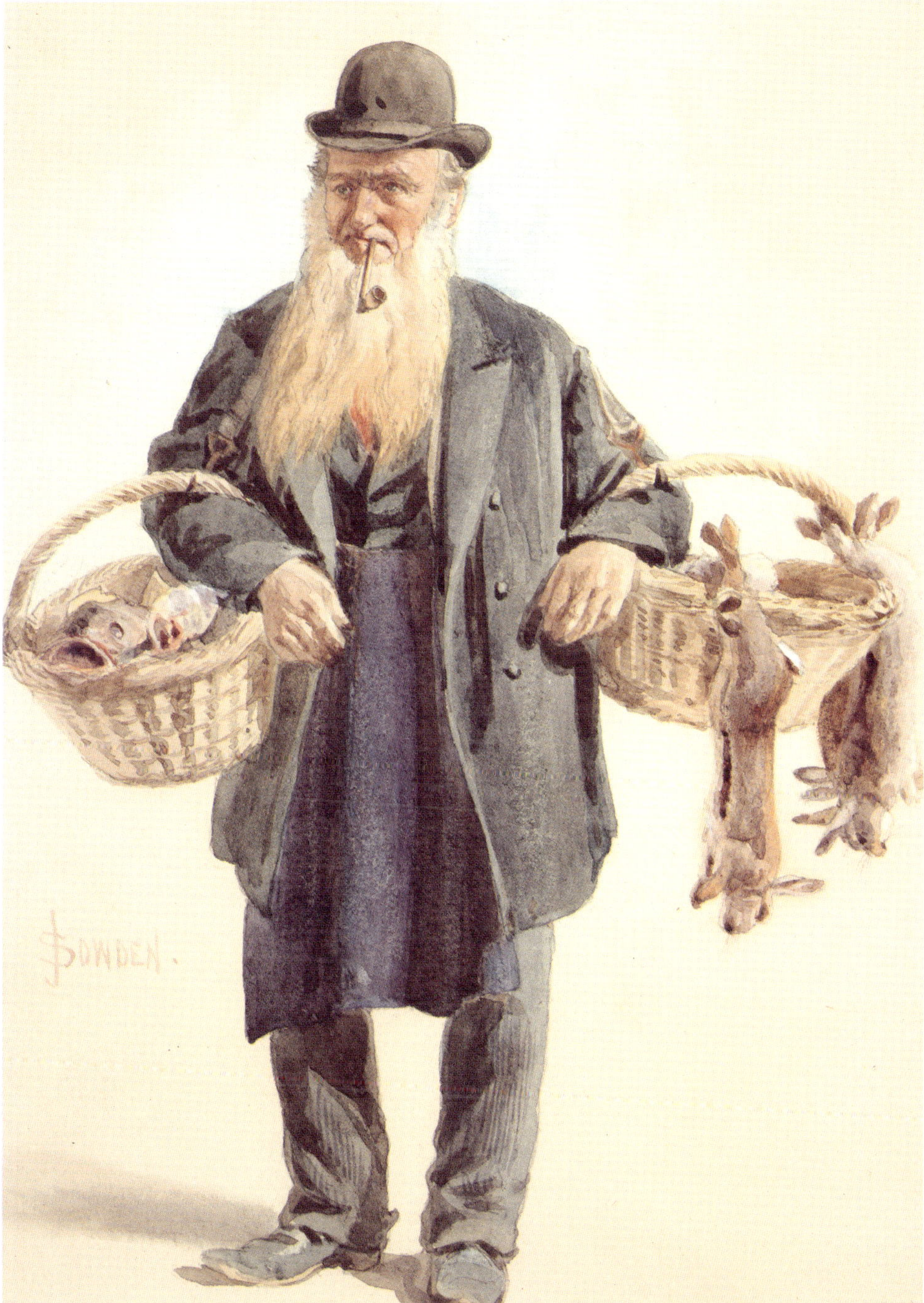
BOWDEN.

16. Sarah Jane LAYCOCK

Perhaps the best known of Victorian Bradford's lady costers was *Cockle Sarah,* born in 1834. In 1873 she had married John Laycock, a vendor of shellfish, who died shortly afterwards and Jane carried on his business. She told Sowden when she sat for him in 1889:

> *there wor a chap after me but I thowt he wor nubbut wantin' me for me cockle rahnd and not for missen.*

She succumbed however, married him and became involved in a bigamy scandal. Undaunted, she continued to sell cockles in the Bowling and Bradford Moor areas and in 1893 remarried one William Garth.

Thousands of Bradfordians of all classes turned up at their wedding at Holy Trinity Church. The crowd was so great it stopped the trams in Leeds Road and caused a massive traffic jam. Sowden tells that:

> *When the bridal party emerged from the church amid loud cheering, rice, peas, horse corn and other similarly indelicate confetti were showered upon the happy pair.*

By 1909 she was widowed again and living with her sister-in-law at 47 Birkshall Lane, where she fell down the cellar steps and broke her neck. She had posed for Sowden in 1889 when she was 55 years of age.

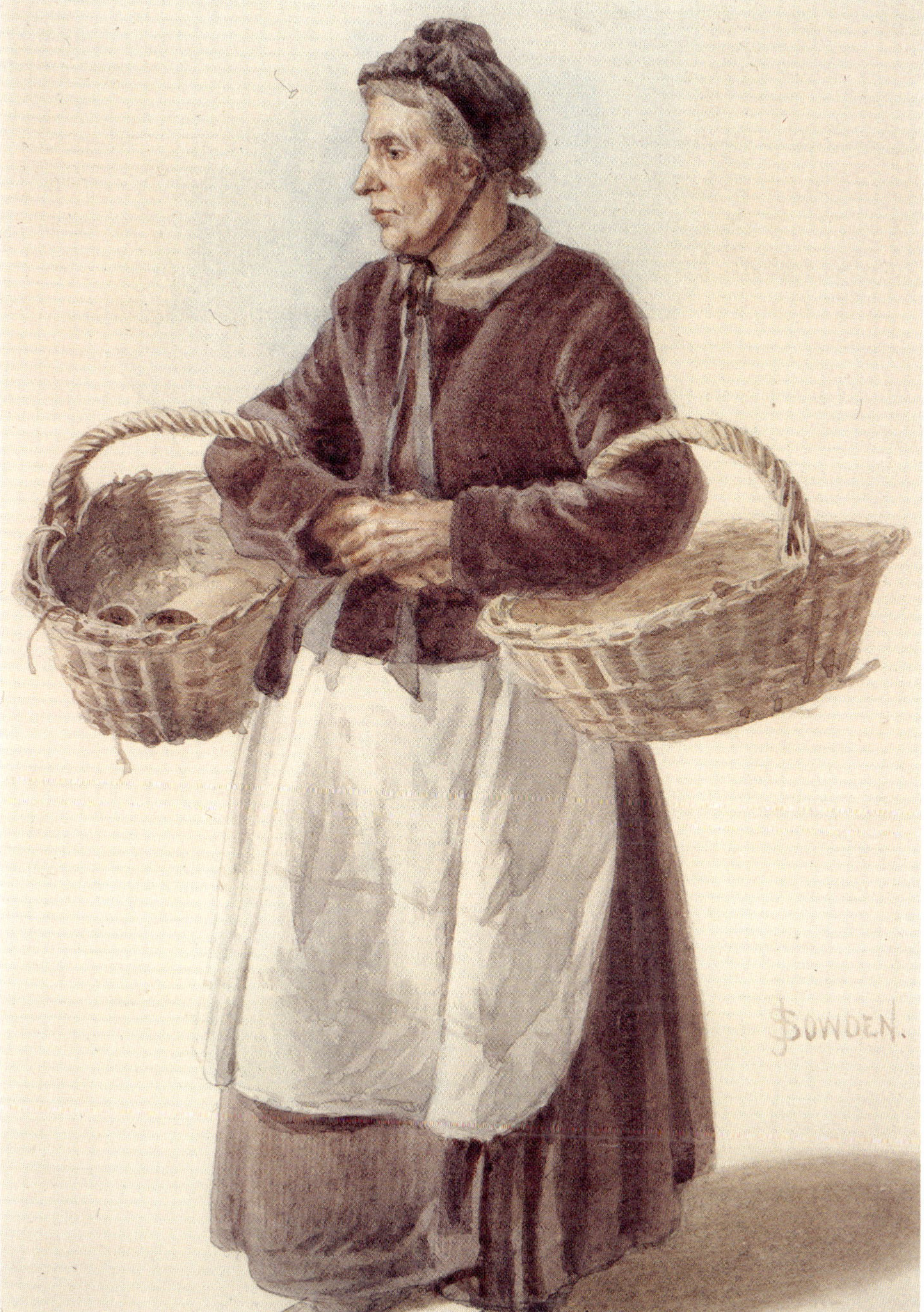
BOWDEN.

17. Benjamin BAIRSTOW

Whistling Tommy Bairstow was christened Benjamin and was of respectable parentage. Bairstow was a Lancastrian who came to Bradford at the age of 15 in 1870. He worked as a porter or general labourer at an ironmongers in the town. He was frequently to be found in the centre of Bradford followed by a gaggle of youths and children who mocked his interminable and enthusiastic whistling. On Jubilee Sunday 1897 he preceded the civic dignitaries in the procession through the town to the Parish Church and whistled the 'Marseillaise' much to the delight of the crowd. When he sat for a marathon four and a half hours in Sowden's studio 22nd November, 1890, Sowden noted that:

> *he whistled selections from the operas and popular airs the whole time.*

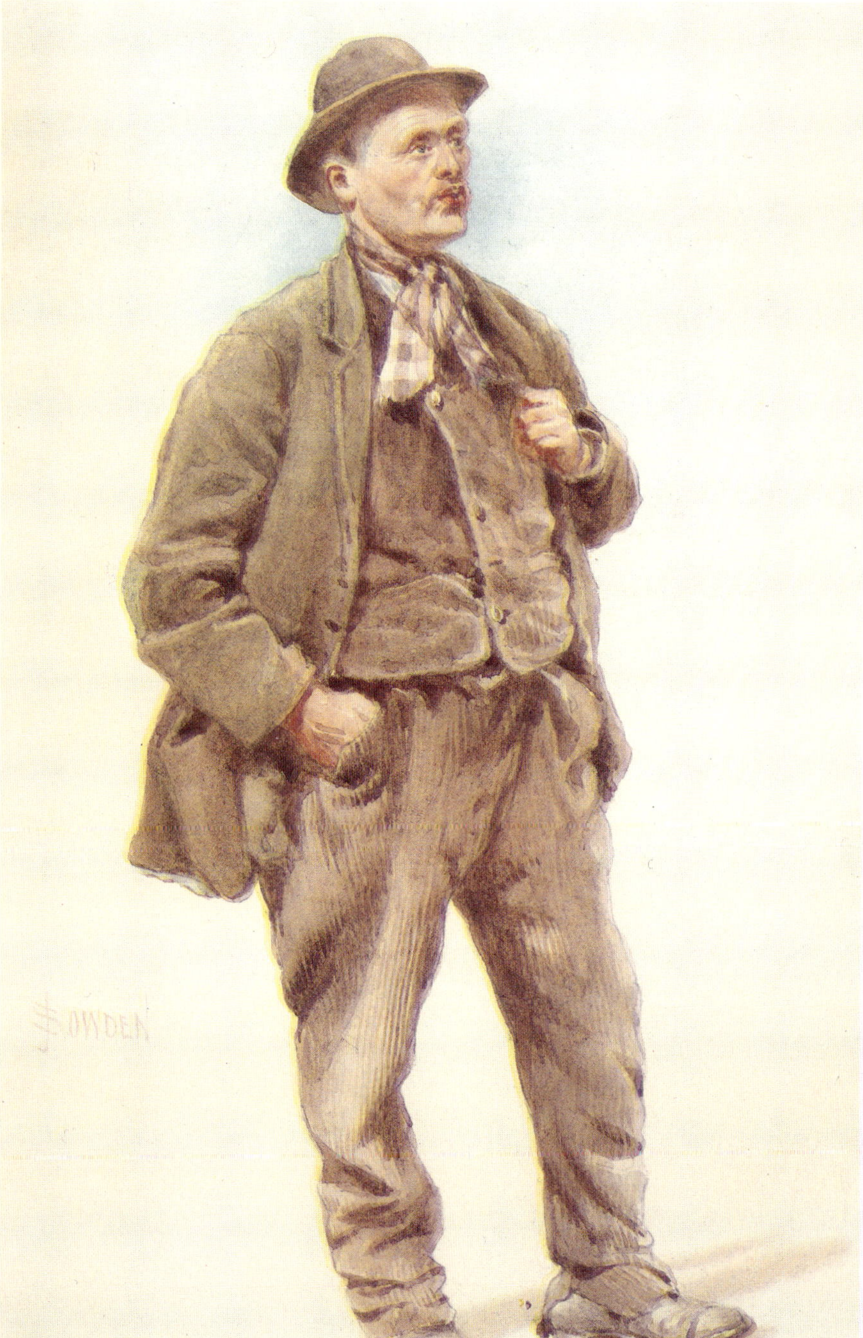
BOWDEN

18. Mary SCHAGER

On 2nd May 1888, Mary Schager posed for John Sowden's afternoon class at the Institute, dressed in a blue skirt and apron, white blouse with full sleeves and her head covered by a red and black scarf. Of Italian origin she told fortunes in the fairs and market places of Victorian Bradford. Beside her in the picture, Sowden provided a blue trestle supporting a small cage of parakeets.

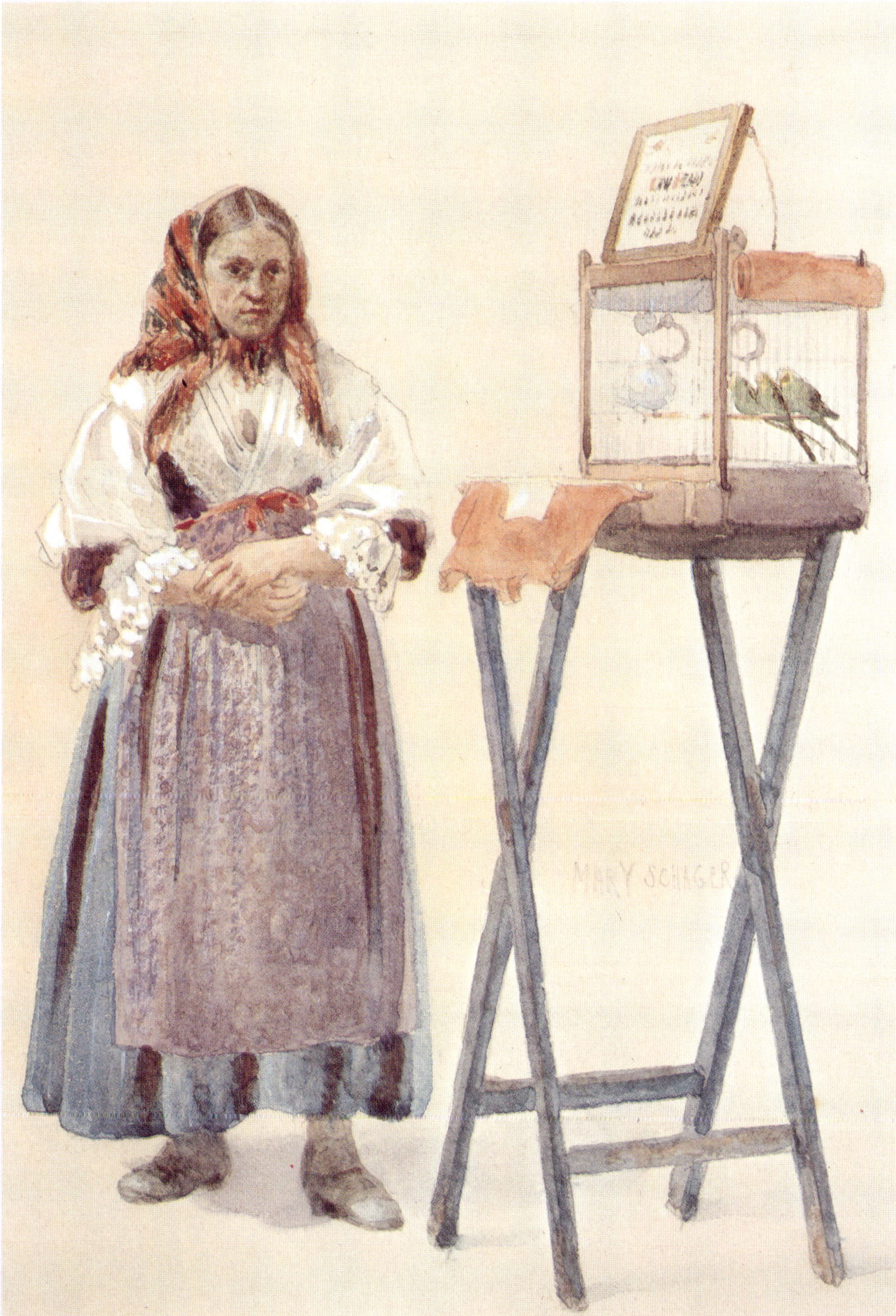
MARY SCHAGER

19. Maria A CERVI

Maria Taglione was born in Costacaldi in July 1868, but in the early 1890s she settled in Bradford along with numerous others of Italian origin. She married Giovanni Cervi in 1896 and for the latter part of her life lived at 13 Paper Hall Street. She played her accordion outside the gates of Peel Park and this is probably where she is posed in Sowden's picture.

20. Andrea VERISCHER

Andrea Verischer was another Bradford street musician who was born in Italy. Wearing clogs, cord trousers and a grey jacket, this youth struggles manfully with the full-size accordion slung round his neck. Like many other street characters, Verischer visited the studio of John Sowden in the summer of 1888, when he was living at Albert Street in Otley Road.

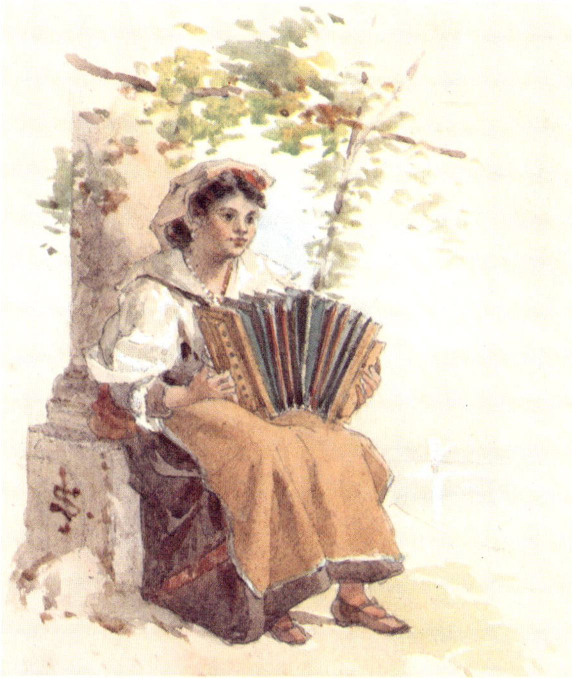

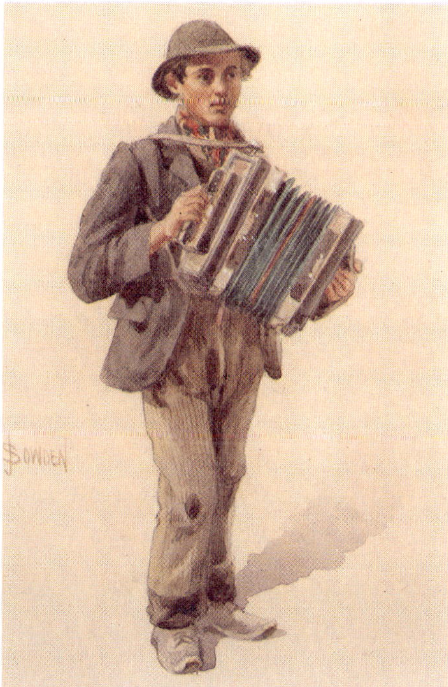
BOWDEN

21. Thomas RYDER

Thomas Ryder was better known to Bradfordians as *t'owd glassner.* In fact Bradford had several travelling glaziers but Irish-born Ryder (1830) and his brother were the best known. Sowden could remember him repairing windows which he himself had broken as a boy in Vicar Lane.

Sowden made several appointments for Ryder to sit in his studio but he broke them all. The artist finally called at Ryder's home in Southgate where his daughter said that she was not going to let him sit unless he was wearing his Sunday best. This would have been no use to Sowden who eventually prevailed on both father and daughter with the promise of a sitting fee of 2 shillings per hour, which was good pay when an average workman was earning less than sixpence per hour. In full working clothes, Ryder eventually posed for Sowden at the Institute studio on 21st October 1890.

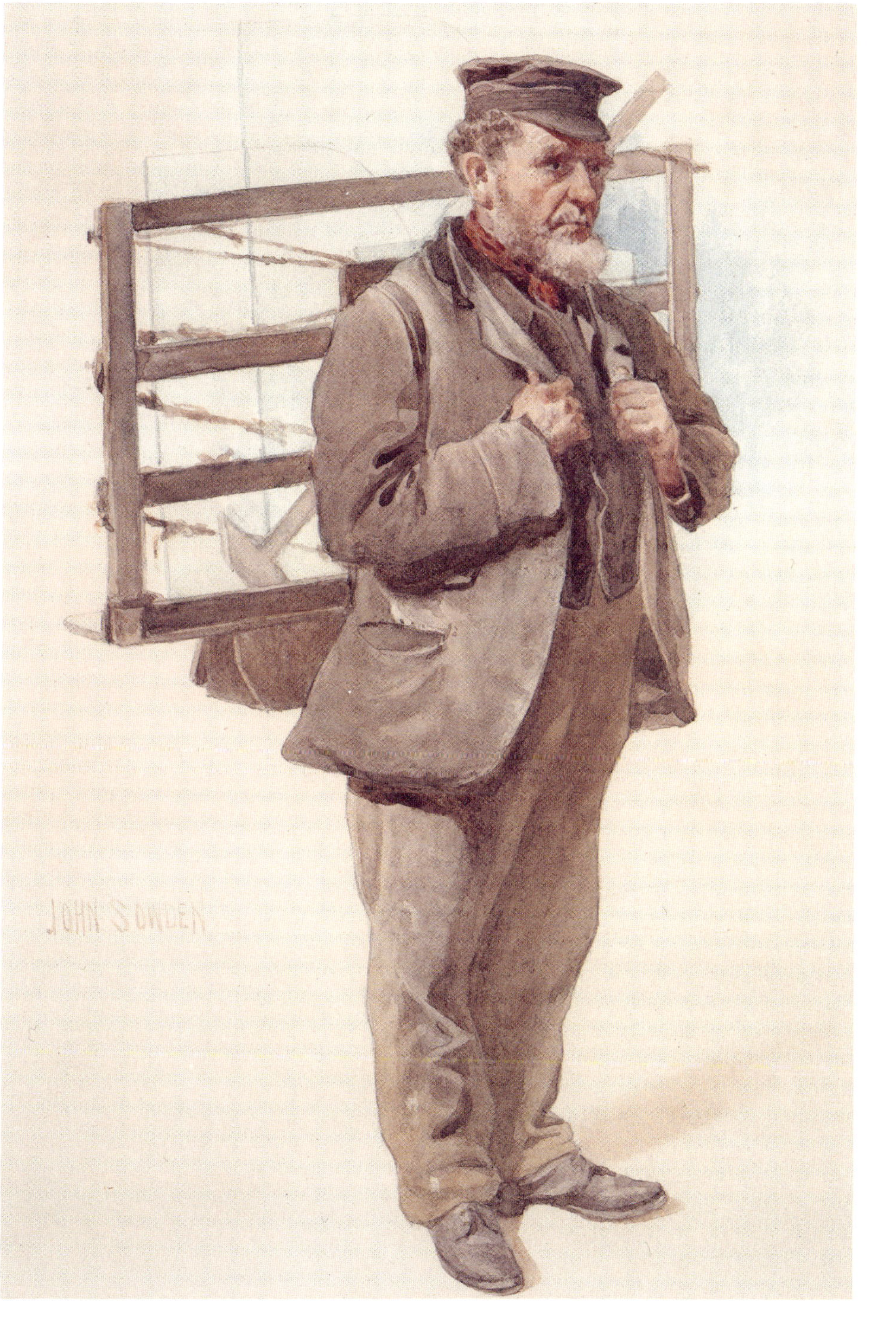
JOHN SOWDEN

22. Fred BONSOR

The son of a Bradford drysalter, Fred Bonsor was educated at Dr Dyson's Academy in Horton. In 1881 he joined the Bradford Football Club and captained them to win the Yorkshire Rugby Union Cup three years later. He was recognised as the finest half back in the country at that time and went on to gain six international caps for England. He was something of a folk hero to the Bradford sporting public and was recognised wherever he went. Unable to hold down regular employment he emigrated to Canada before the end of the century.

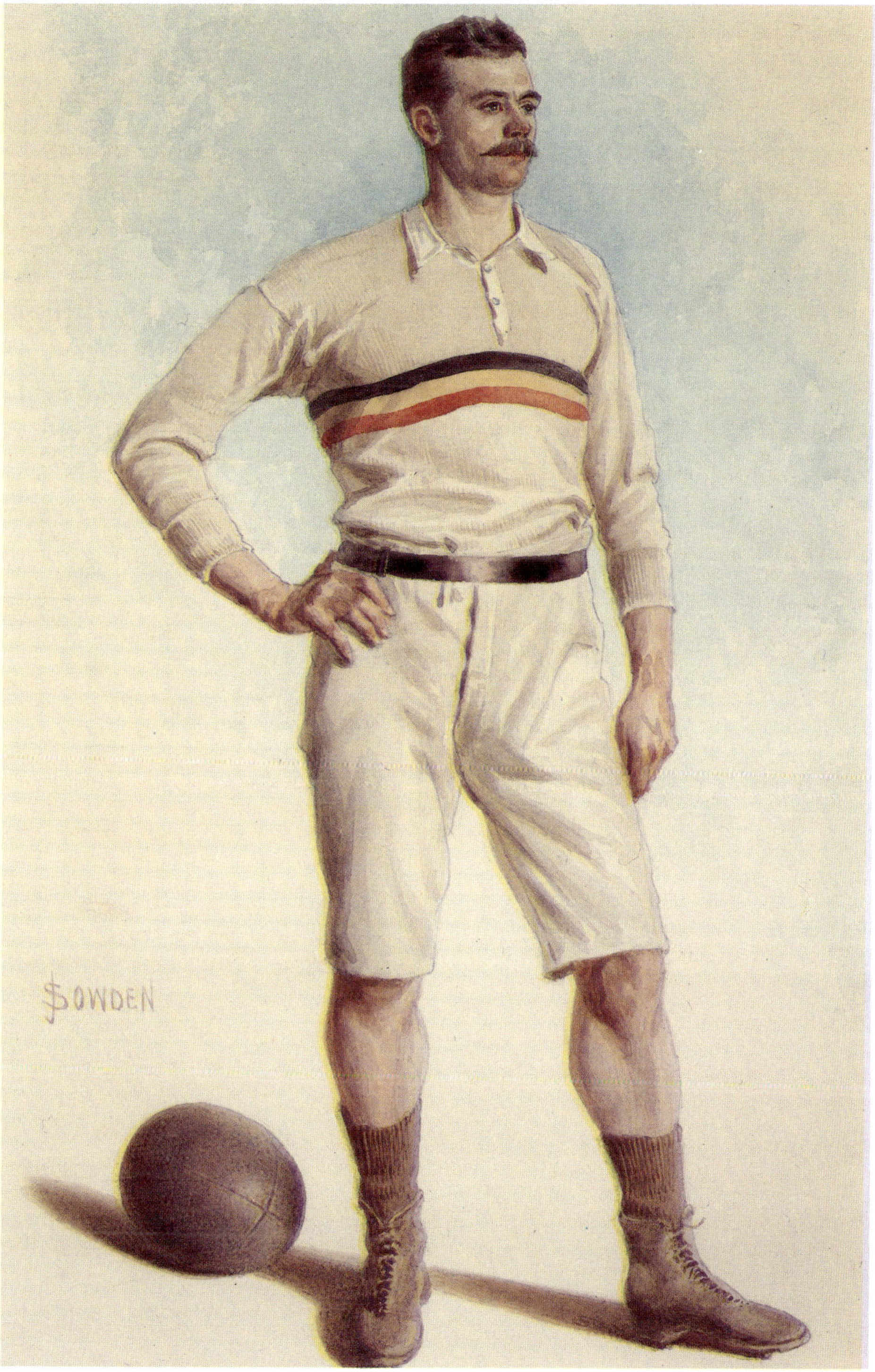
BOWDEN

23. Mary O'BRIEN

Mary had been a hawker of pots since she arrived from Ireland in 1845 at the age of 24. The Irish had been a distinct ethnic minority in Bradford since the 1820's but migration to West Yorkshire was particularly intense following the Irish electoral laws in 1829, and also in the period 1831-45, before the Great Famine. Many of these immigrants came from peasant communities in the west of Ireland, although many also came from Queens County with its tradition of cloth making. Mary O'Brien emigrated at this time but without textile skills, so she resorted to the hawking of pots and pans and was familiarly known as *Pot Mary.* You will note she sports a large wedding ring.

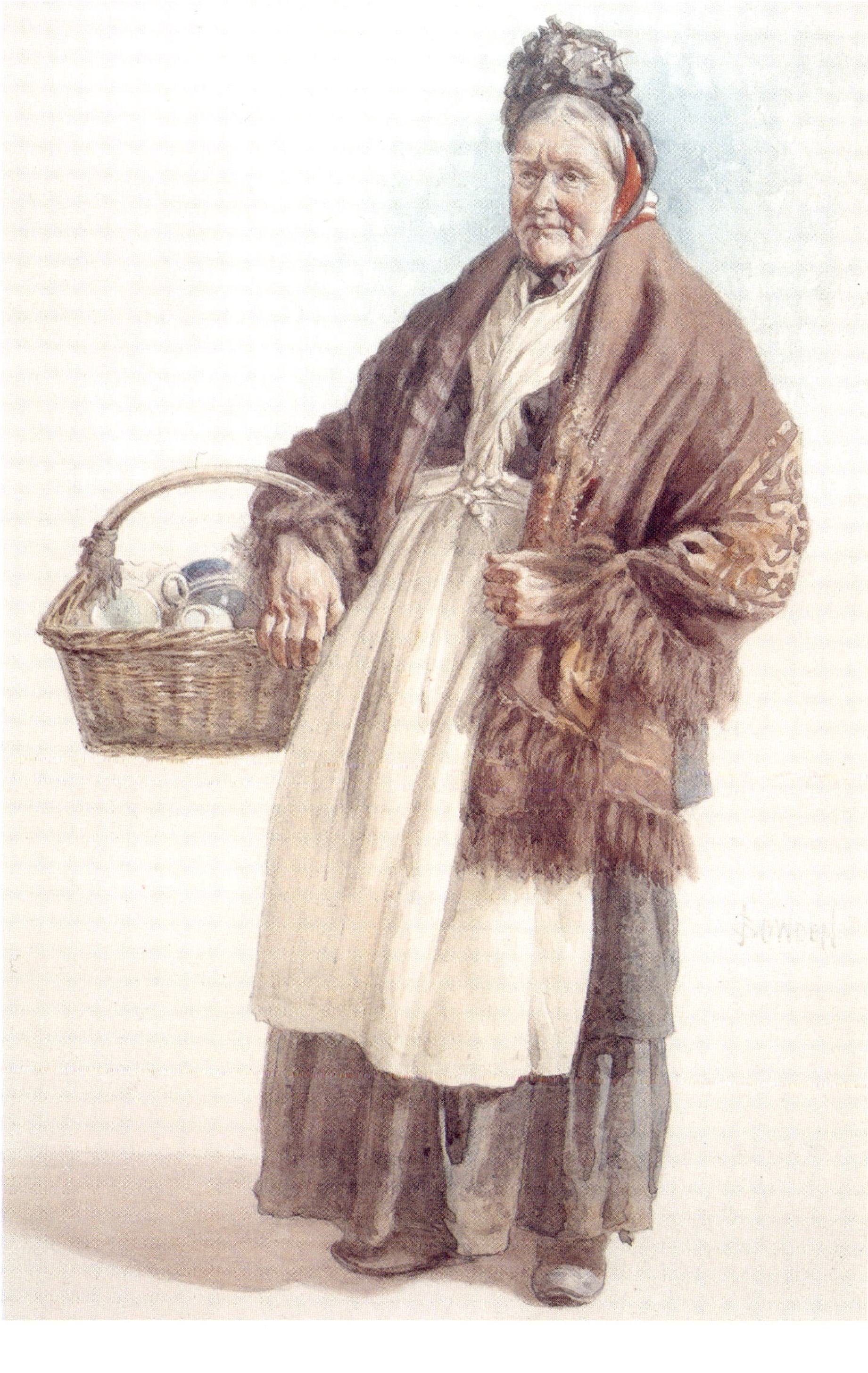

24. Thomas BOTTOMLEY

Well known to the criminal classes of the town as *Tom Bott,* Police Constable Bottomley's main beat was in the Manningham area, where he was well known for quiet sensitive policing, for example:

"If tha don't go hoam to thi wife and bairns a sal hev to run tha in". This was probably successful for it is said he never had a case reach the courts in thirty years.

By the time of his portrait in 1890, Bottomley was one of 256 constables in the Bradford City Police Force under the Chief Constableship of James Withers. As suburban police stations opened at Manningham, Great Horton, Bowling, Allerton and Heaton, the force increased accordingly, and Bottomley's conditions of service improved considerably.

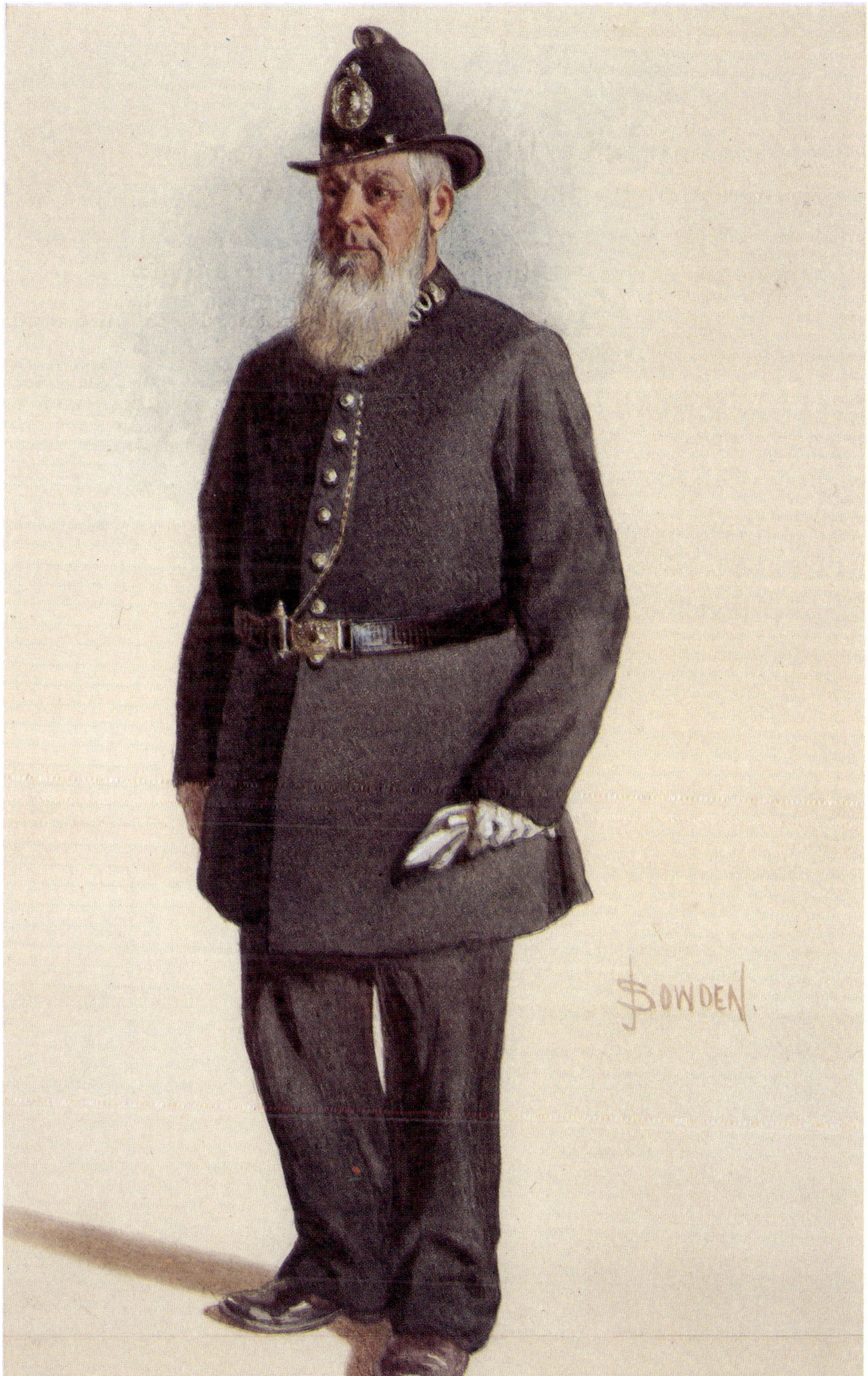
BOWDEN

25. William HOLMES

One of Bradford's oldest itinerants (91 years), Holmes played his mouth organ outside the pubs and theatres of the town centre. When he sat for Sowden just before Christmas in 1888 he told the artist that his early life had been spent as a railway labourer. Initially he had worked in Devon and Cornwall and later spent some time as a platelayer in Russia. In 1850 he retired with a nest egg of £2,000 which he gave to his son to open a grocer's shop in the town. Shortly afterwards Holmes suffered a stroke and ended up in the Bradford Workhouse, his son having cleared off to Australia never to be heard from again. Forty years later this resilient old man still walked the streets of Bradford, crippled, impoverished, but fiercely independent.

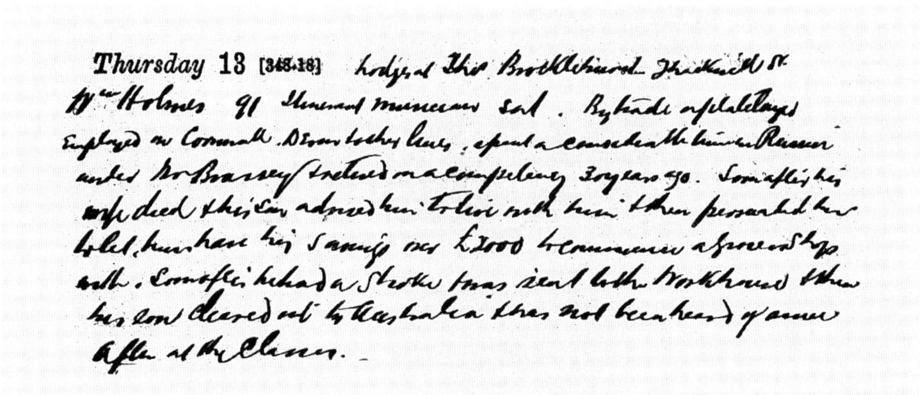
Thursday 13 [348-18] Lodged Thos. Brocklehurst Thickwood St. Wm Holmes 91 Itinerant musician sat. By trade a platelayer employed in Cornwall Devon & other lines, spent a considerable time in Russia under Mr Brassey & retired on a competency 30 years ago. Soon after his wife died & his son advised him to live with him & then persuaded him to let him have his savings over £2000 to commence a grocer's shop with. Soon after he had a stroke & was sent to the Workhouse & then his son cleared out to Australia & has not been heard of since. After at the Classes. –

John Sowden's diary. Thursday 13th December, 1888.

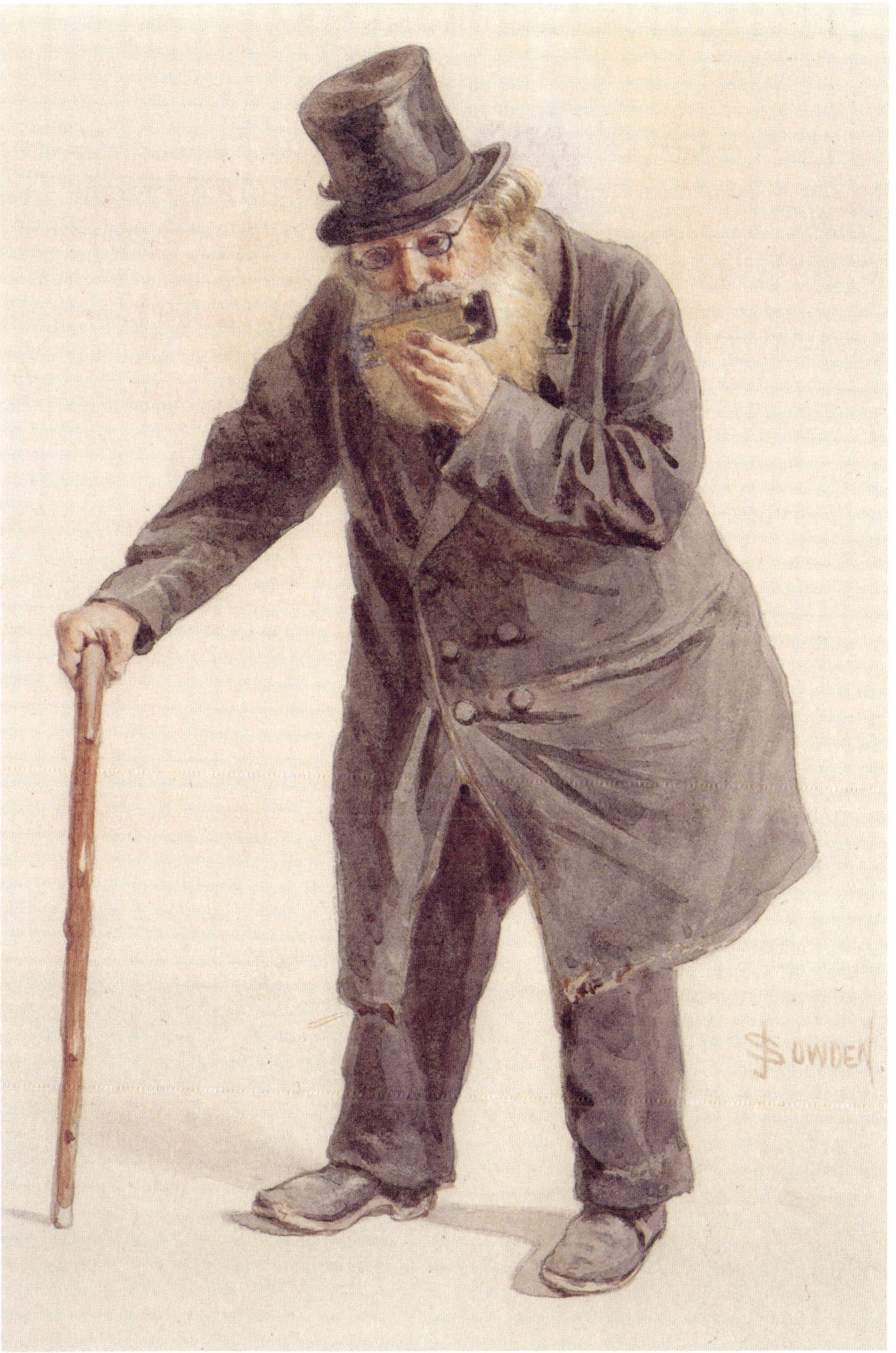

26. John ROSS

John Ross was better known to his contemporaries as *Cheap John* for the cheapness of his small wares, particularly brooms and brushes. He had hawked these goods around the town since 1851. Shortly before he had worked as a labourer in a local stone quarry. There, a huge stone fell upon his head, taking out one of his eyes and breaking his hip. For two years he was hospitalised at the Bradford Workhouse. When Ross, then aged 77, left Sowden's studio on 26th May 1888 the artist *patrolled around the town for tomorrow's classes and found a blind organette player in Kirkgate, a quack doctor and George Pinchin the celery man. Afterwards went to the Club.*

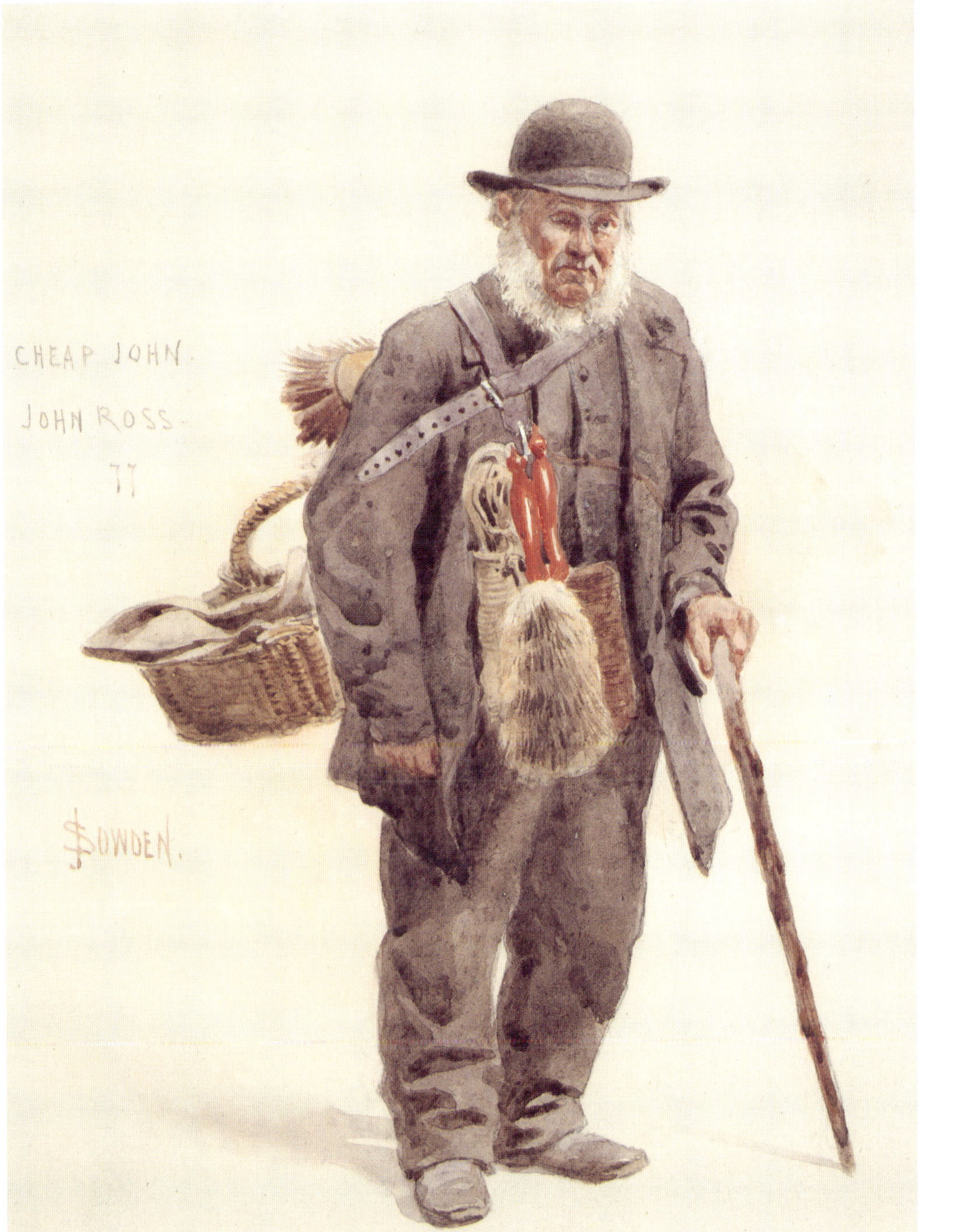
CHEAP JOHN.
JOHN ROSS.
77
BOWDEN.

27. Jimmie HEY

James Hey was born in 1865 and died shortly after his portrait was painted in 1909. This is one of several of the portraits completed by Sowden between 1909 and 1914 when he was getting old. It shows a diminutive figure in a badly fitting suit of tails, holding a cue rest and standing beside a billiard table. Billiards was a favourite pastime of the artist. Every Saturday night for the last thirty years of his life he could be found round the billiard table at the Bradford Liberal Club, impeccably dressed and with a cigar in hand. Perhaps Hey was the steward there?

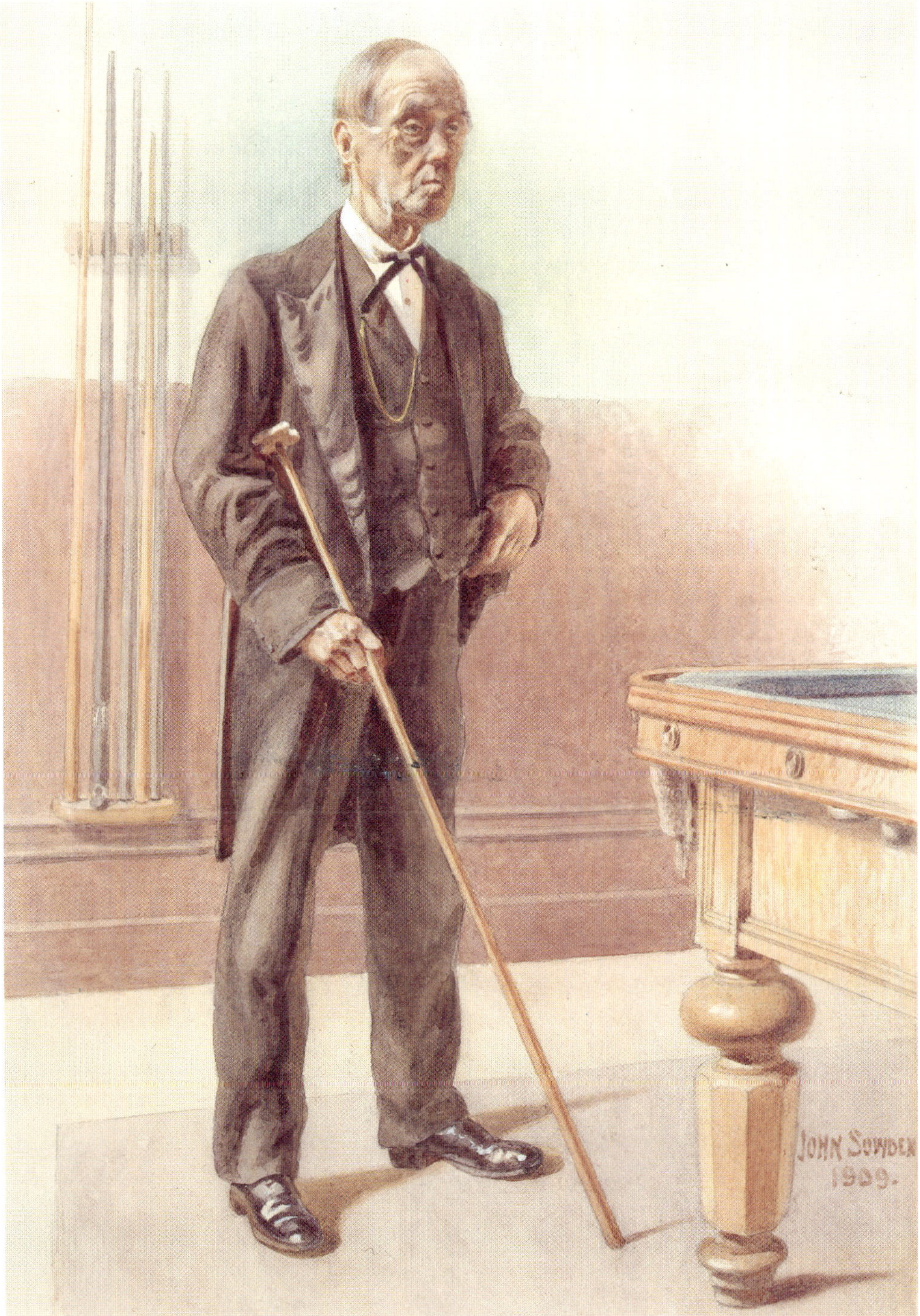
JOHN SOWDEN
1909.

28. George PINCHIN

George Pinchin posed for Sowden's morning model class in May 1888 when he was 65 years of age. He had sold celery at Bradford Green Market, near Rawson Square, every Saturday for thirty five years. Only a fortnight before sitting for Sowden he had sold 1,200 sticks of celery (weighing 14cwt) in one week "and generally sells 1,000 sticks a week during the season". Pinchin was a native of Kidderminster.

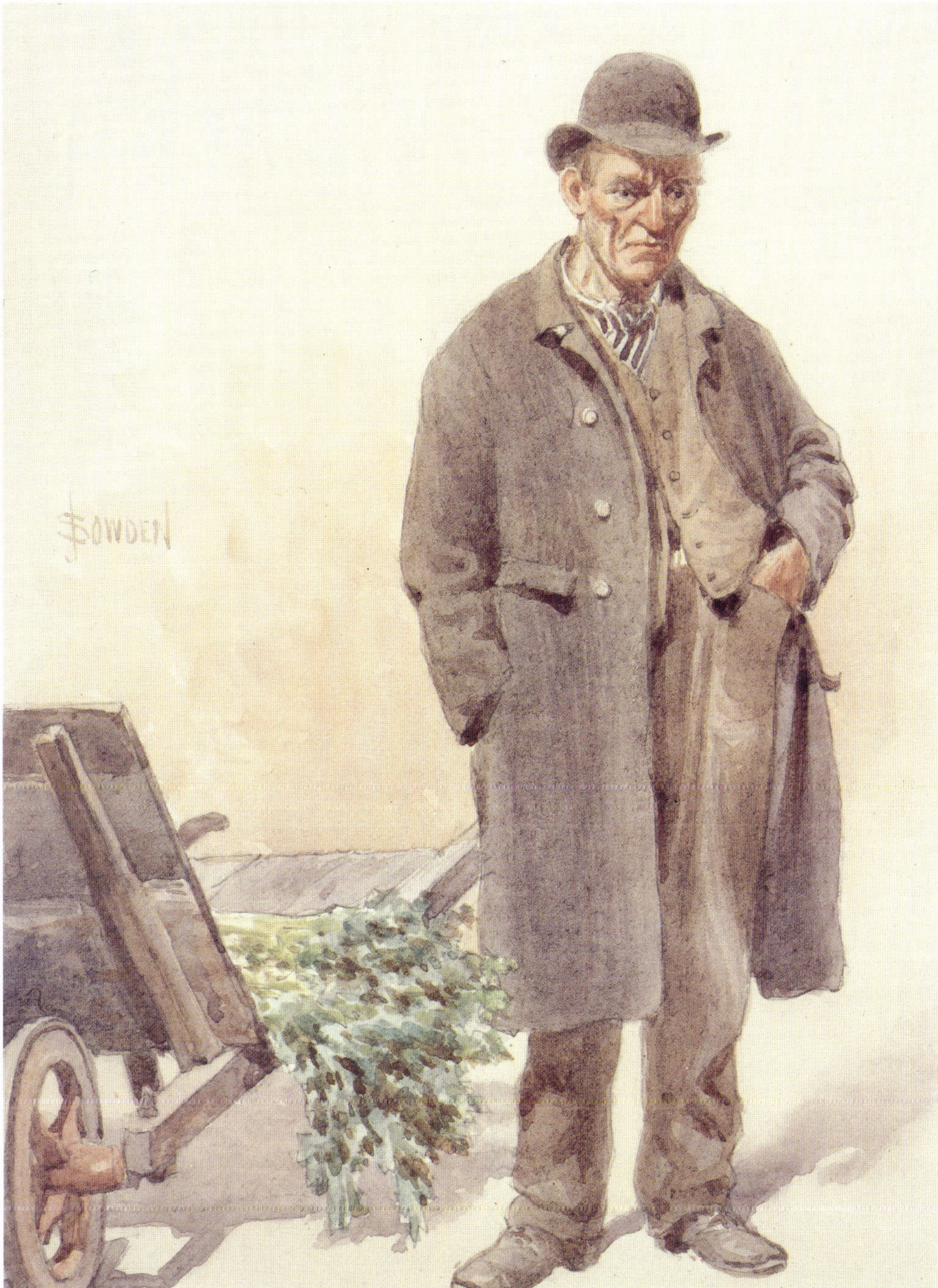
BOWDEN

29. Thomas JACKSON

Old Tom, as he was better known, sat down in Sowden's studio at the ripe old age of 73. Sowden had spent the whole of 3rd May 1888 searching for a suitable model for his afternoon class and was particularly pleased to persuade Thomas Jackson to pose for his students. His bright and distinctive clothing, brown cord trousers, black and green coat and bright red neckerchief, offered the would-be artists much potential.

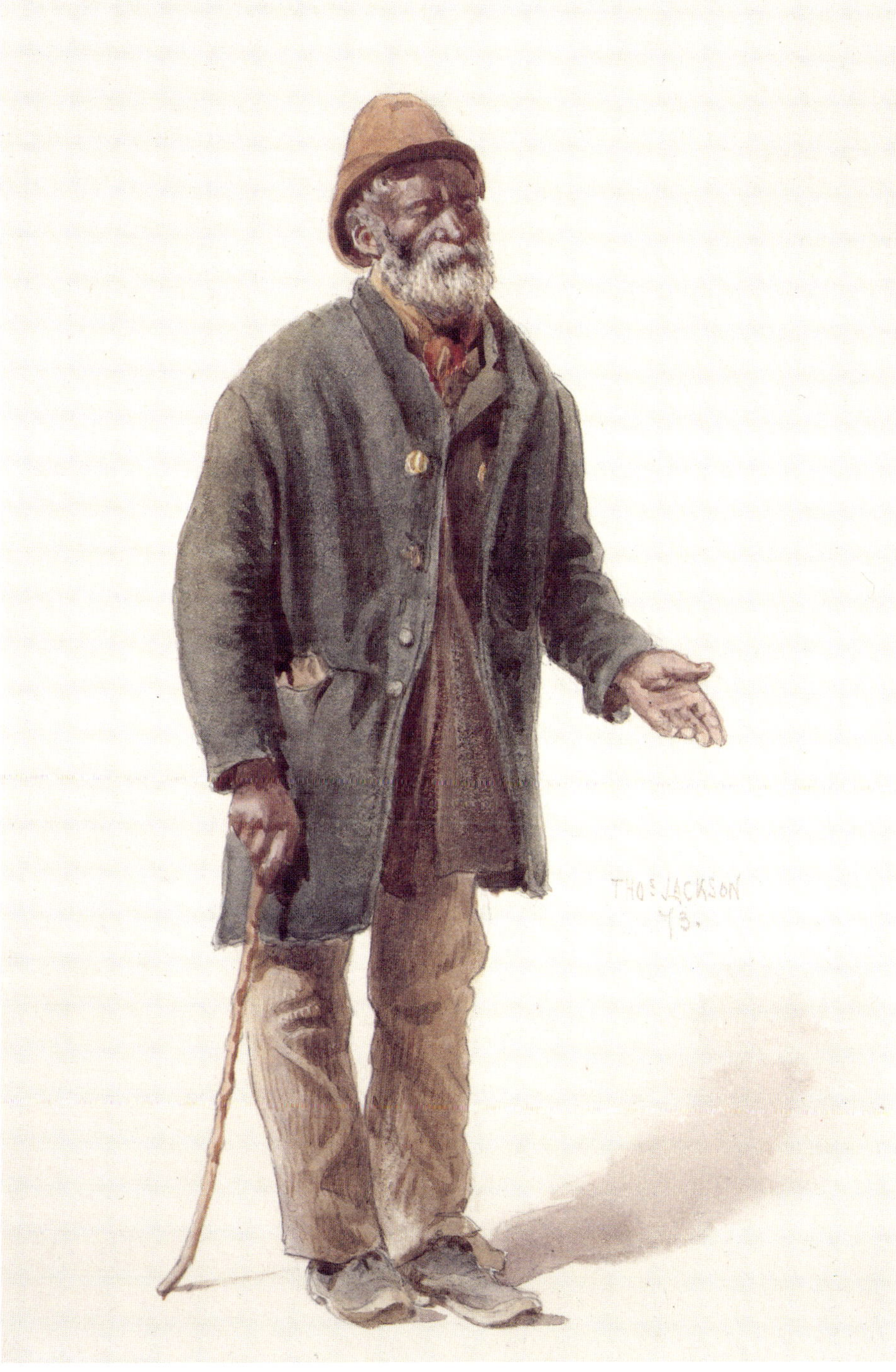
THOs JACKSON
73.

30. Tom JONES

This shabbily dressed eleven year old boy wandered the streets of Bradford selling matches. He actually sat for Sowden in the summer of 1888 when women and girls of Jones' age were striking in the East End of London for better working conditions in the match-making business of Bryant & May. Their seemingly hopeless cause was championed by Annie Besant, a socialist, whose weekly newspaper brought the match girls' plight into the public eye. At first the company refused to give in to the girls' demands but the public outcry against them forced a change of heart and compelled the firm to grant concessions.

The waif Jones probably knew little of this major landmark in labour history and cared even less, but to others, like John Burns and Tom Mann, the success of the London match girls gave a tremendous boost to unionism for the unskilled worker.

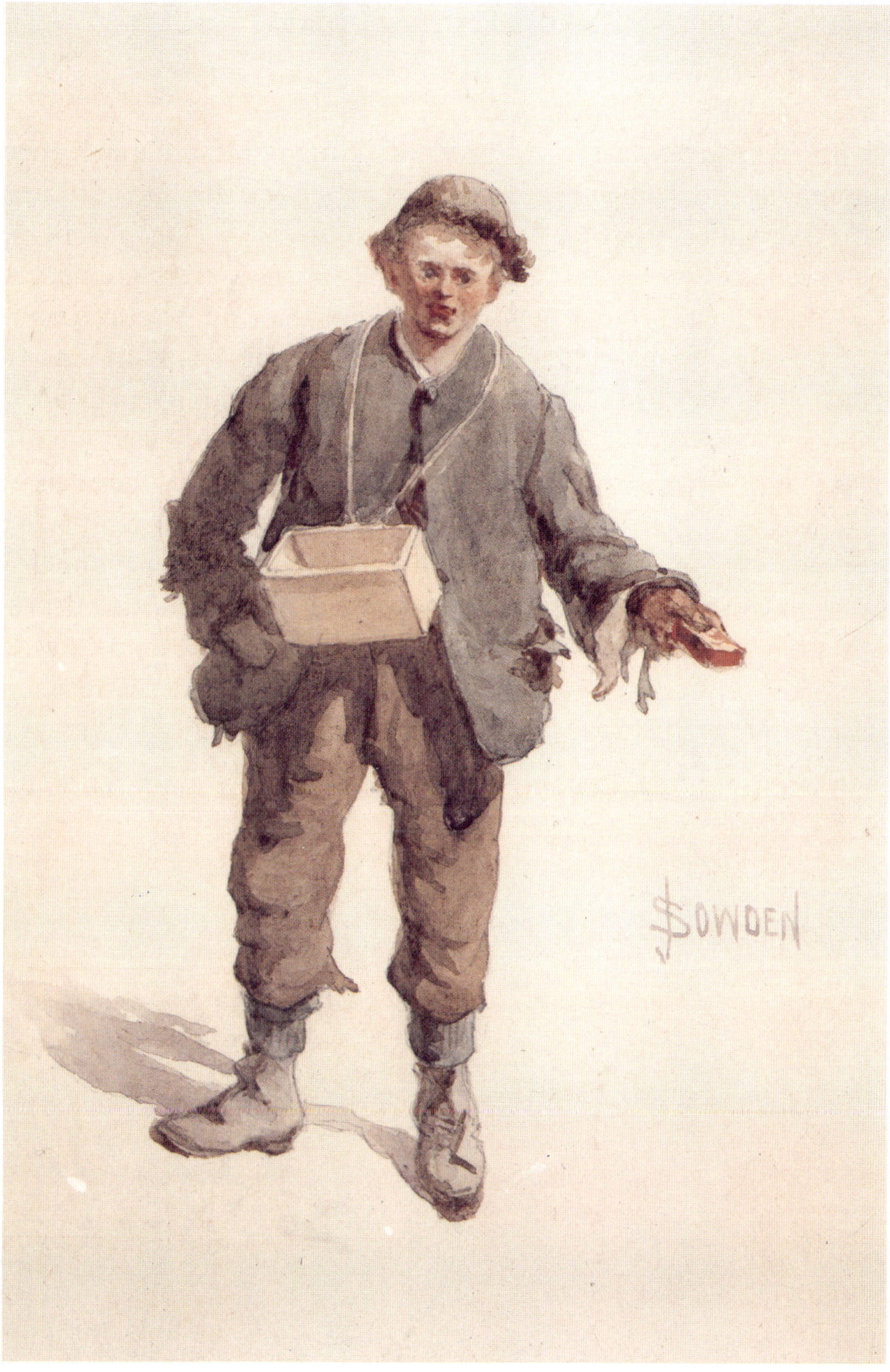
SBOWDEN

31. Henry MADEN

From his immaculate top hat to his shiny black boots Henry Maden was every inch Bradford's proudest cabman. One of three cabmen painted by John Sowden, Maden was, by far and away, the best known. He and his three fine horses were stationed at 'Baltimore', a rank just beyond Queens Road on Manningham Lane. From there, Maden gave first class service to the many wealthy industrialists, millowners and landed families who lived in that exclusive neighbourhood of Bradford. He was their first choice to escort their precocious children to parties or themselves on weekend trips into Wharfedale. For a quarter of a century he worked a seven day week; a yellow woollen muffler round his throat in winter and sporting a light suit and 'boater' in summer.

Maden is immortalised in this painting by Sowden but he was also mentioned in the memoirs of Sir William Rothenstein when writing of family life in Manningham in the high Victorian period.

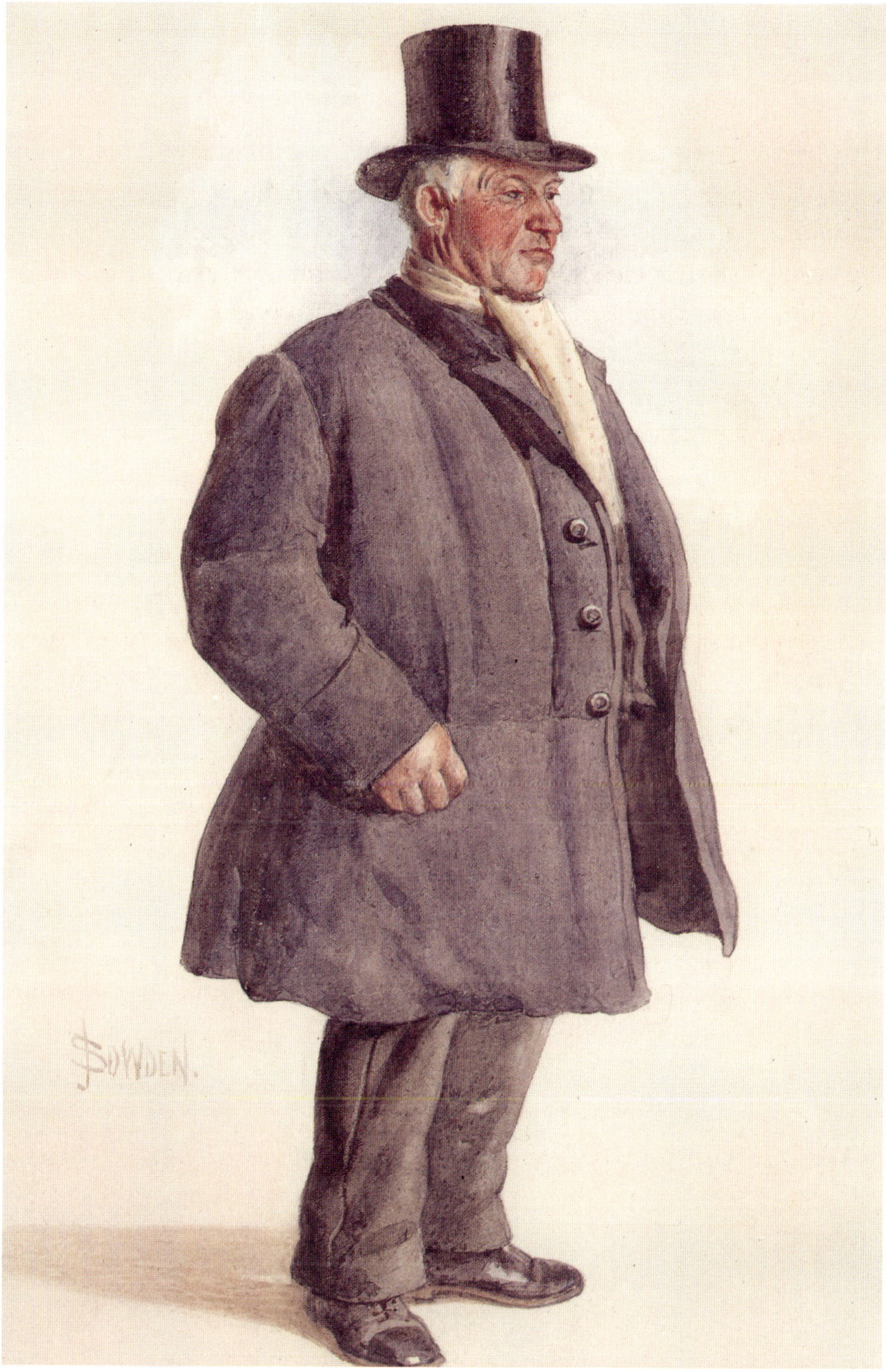
BOWDEN.

32. Annie WALKER

This twelve year old flower seller crept coyly into Sowden's studio in April 1888. Annie lived at 13 Longlands Street, in one of Bradford's notorious slum quarters. Of Longland Street, near Westgate, a contemporary wrote:

> *In Longlands Street a young girl wearing a mill skirt sat near the door. She had hurriedly swallowed her breakfast that she might devote a few minutes towards the completion of a stocking which was half-knitted. The mother was cleaning up the hearth. The former earned her ten shillings a week, the latter five or six as a washerwoman. Neither enjoyed good health and the temporary collapse of either was fatal indeed to the family, comprising six souls all told and the two frail creatures of whom I have just spoken were the breadwinners.*

This is a sharp reminder of the poverty, misery and squalor which beset the lives of many of Sowden's characters. To sit doing nothing in his warm and welcoming studio and be paid two shillings an hour for the privilege was, for many of the characters, a most welcome break from the daily round of hunger, ill health, hard work and grinding poverty. We should not overlook this fact as we sentimentalise on Sowden's little 'primrose dame'.

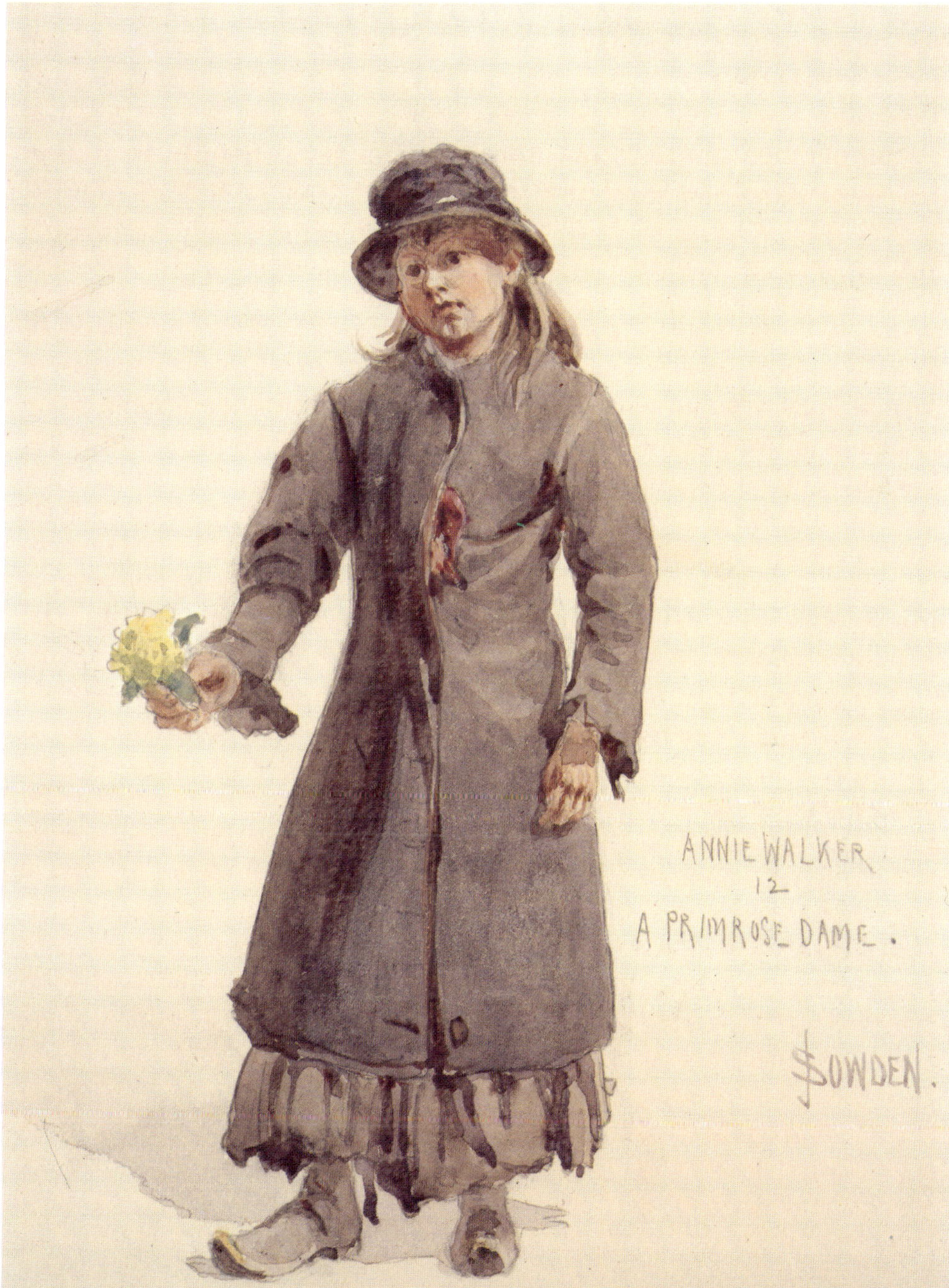
ANNIE WALKER
12
A PRIMROSE DAME.
SOWDEN.

33. John STANNARD

A relative newcomer to Bradford, Stannard had only lived in the town (in Westgate) since 1876. He was a native of Kidderminster and had been blind since the age of 16 as a result of smallpox. He first visited Sowden's studio at the end of May 1888. He is dressed in a billycock hat, a brown coat and matching waistcoat. Around his neck is the usual begging tin and a large board supporting two large books from which he is reading by the use of his fingers.

A contemporary of Sowden's writing of a visit into the poverty corners of Westgate noted:

> *a blind man. He wore a yellow mixture dust coat, sadly worn, a pair of trousers much too short for him .... What must it be I ask to one blind, inform and aged, to be compelled day after day to drift in perpetual darkness from shop to shop from public house in the hope of selling a pound or two of tobacco and at the week end to find that for this wandering the return is half a crown.*

Unfortunately, this was the lot of many of Bradford's blind people.

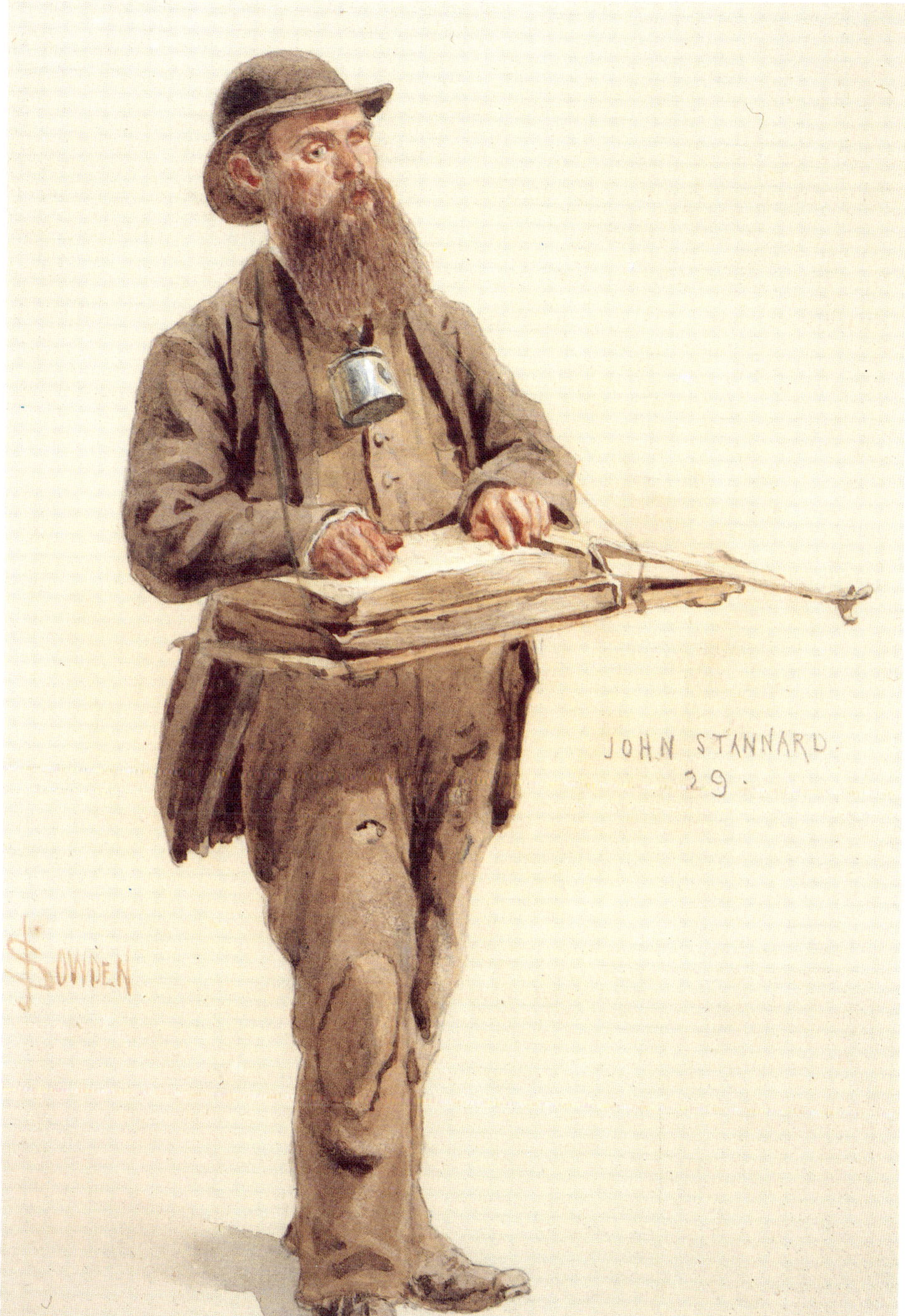
JOHN STANNARD
29.
SOWDEN

34. Sarah SMITH

Yet another of Bradford's blind community, Sarah had travelled in Wales but had been born at Tadcaster in 1833. She lost the use of her eyes at the age of 40. She had a regular begging 'patch' on the steps leading to Stott Hill near the Parish Church. She sat for Sowden on 15th May 1888.

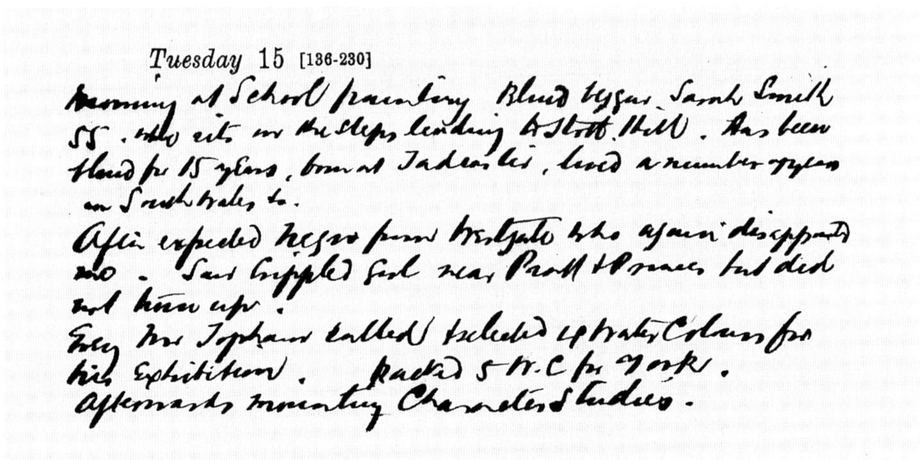
Tuesday 15 [136-230]
Morning at School painting Blind beggar Sarah Smith
55. who sits on the steps leading to Stott Hill. Has been
blind for 15 years, born at Tadcaster, lived a number of years
in South Wales &c.
After expected negro from Westgate who again disappointed
me. Saw Crippled girl near Pratt & Prince's but did
not know her.
Evening Mr Topham called & selected 4 Water Colours for
his Exhibition. Packed 5 W.C for York.
Afterwards mounting Character Studies.

John Sowden's diary. Tuesday 15th May, 1888.

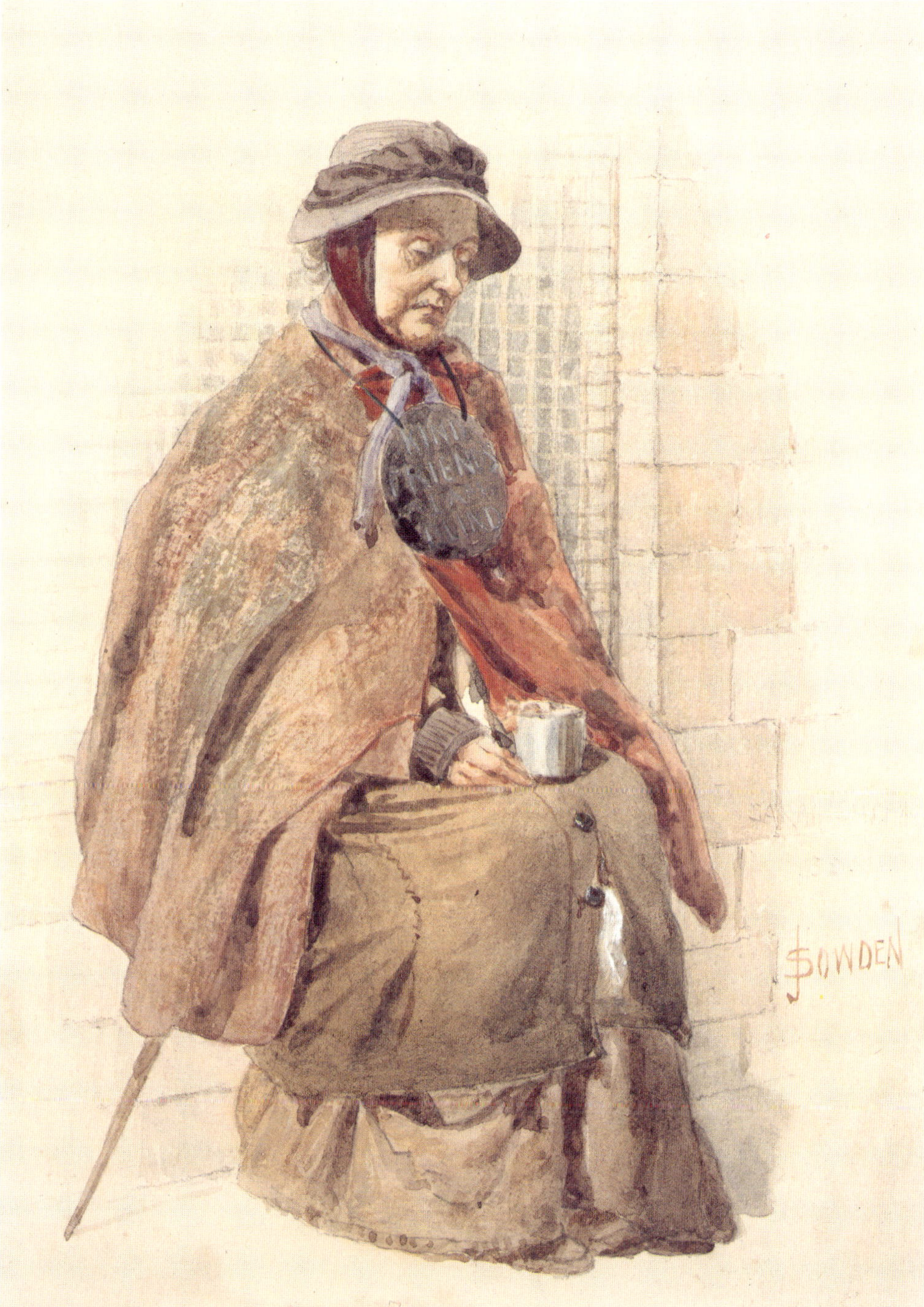

35. John DOBBY

Here is the very spirit of Victorian respectability and self help: John Dobby was one of Bradford's most successful tradesmen. He was born in Wilsden, on the outskirts of Bradford, in 1837 and at the age of fourteen was apprenticed to the Bradford butcher William Greetham.

Nine years later he began business on his own account and for fifty years his became the principal butchering business in the district. In 1887 he entered politics serving as a Conservative councillor in the Bradford Moor Ward. He became Chairman of the Yorkshire Butchers Hide & Skin Company and was one of the founders of the Municipal Insurance Fund. He died on the eve of the First World War. He posed for Sowden at the Institute studio between 8th-15th July 1890.

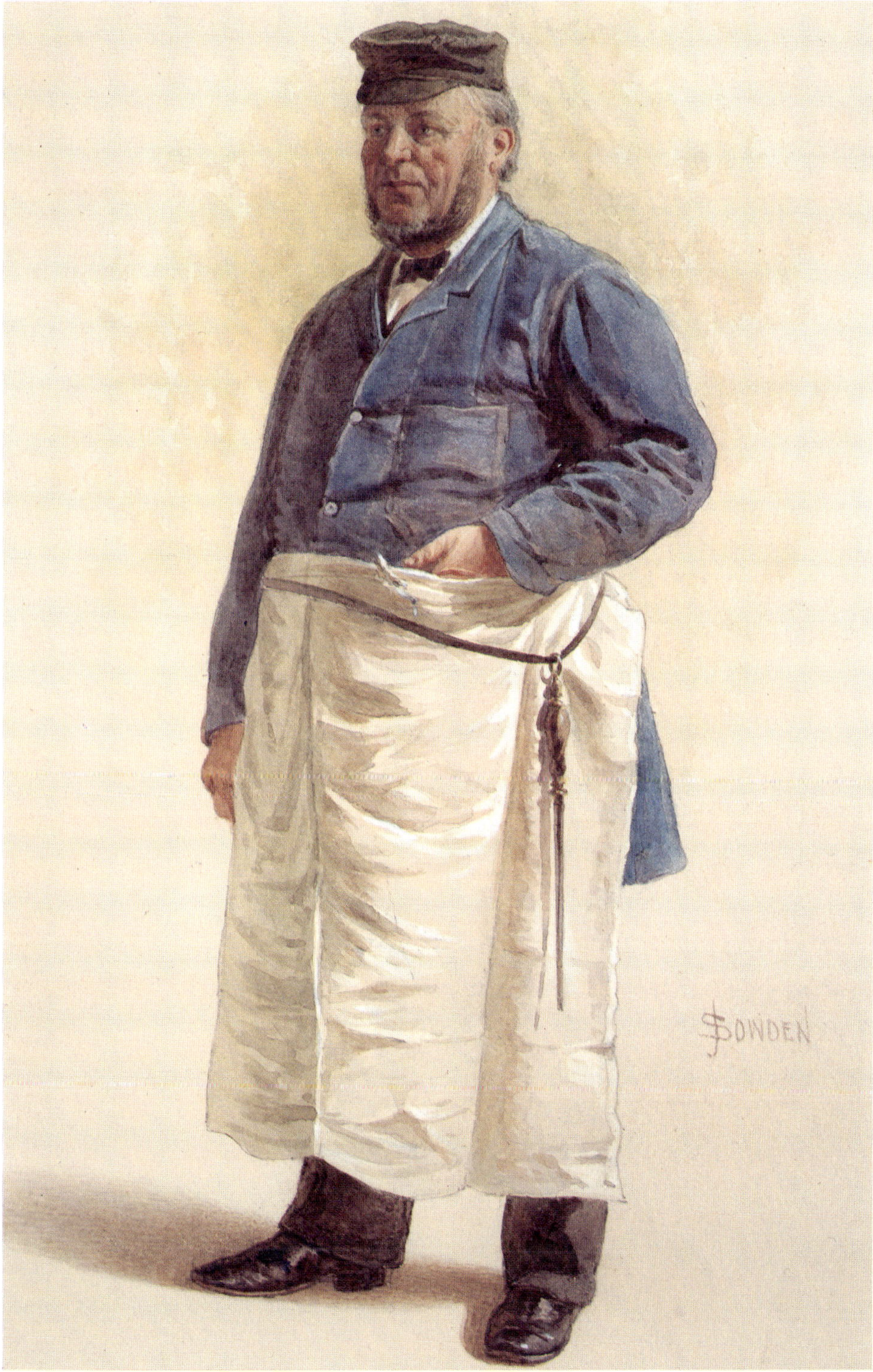
BOWDEN

36. John Grose FAWBERT

Sowden's diary for 2nd May 1888 reads:

> *At Morning Class. Figure day. Expected blind man from Darley Street but did not come. Waited nearly an hour and afterwards fetched a crippled and ragged newsboy in. Had dinner at Club.*

Although he is not named, it is highly likely that Sowden's subject for that day was the unfortunate John Grose Fawbert who had lost his right foot as the painting shows.

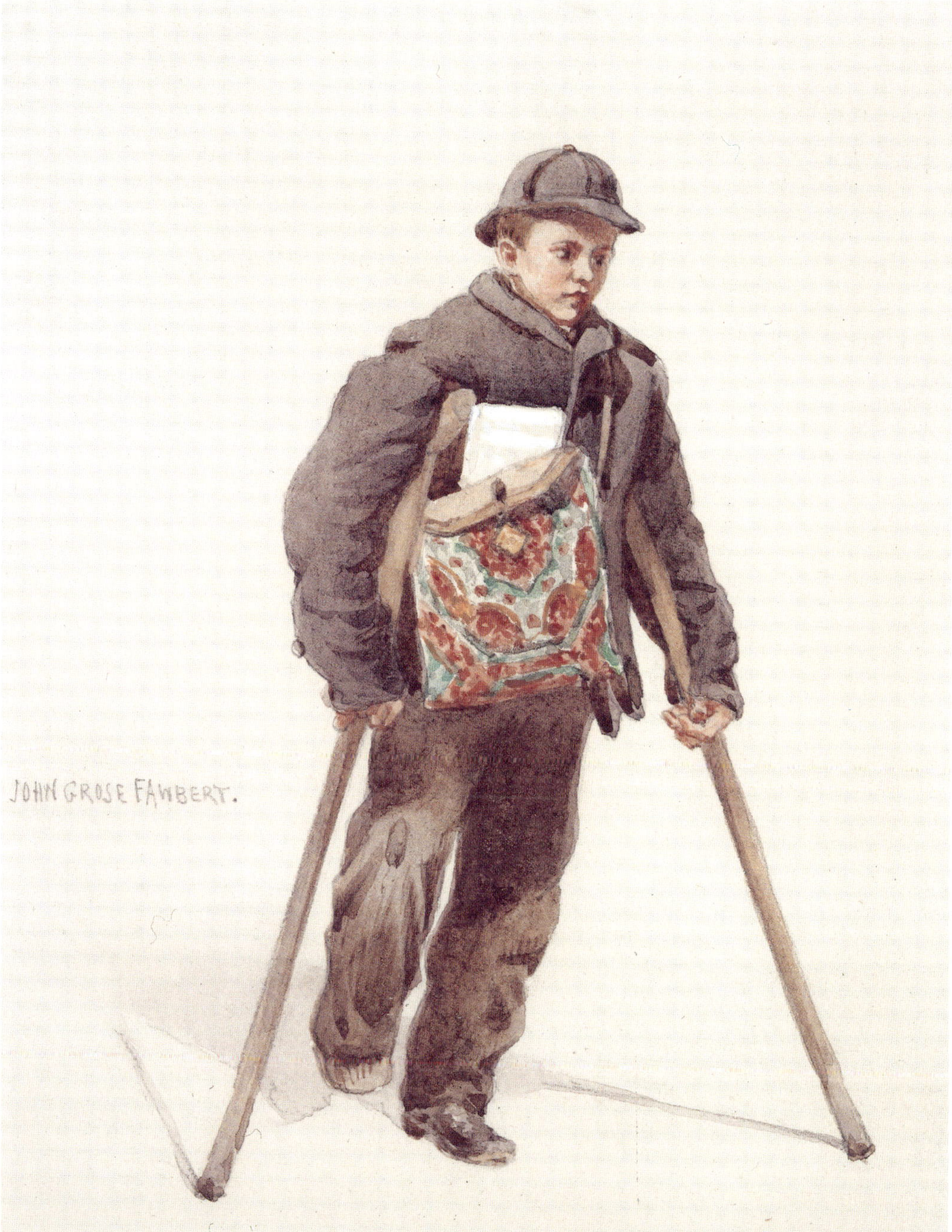
JOHN GROSE FAWBERT.

37. John FEELY

At 75 years of age, John Feely was still in full time employment as a labourer, perhaps the oldest in Bradford (where he had lived since 1838). However, when trade was slack, old John made himself a living (like several others, e.g. John Fawcett and John Hart) as a hawker of oranges. John posed for Sowden's sketching club on 10th May 1888.

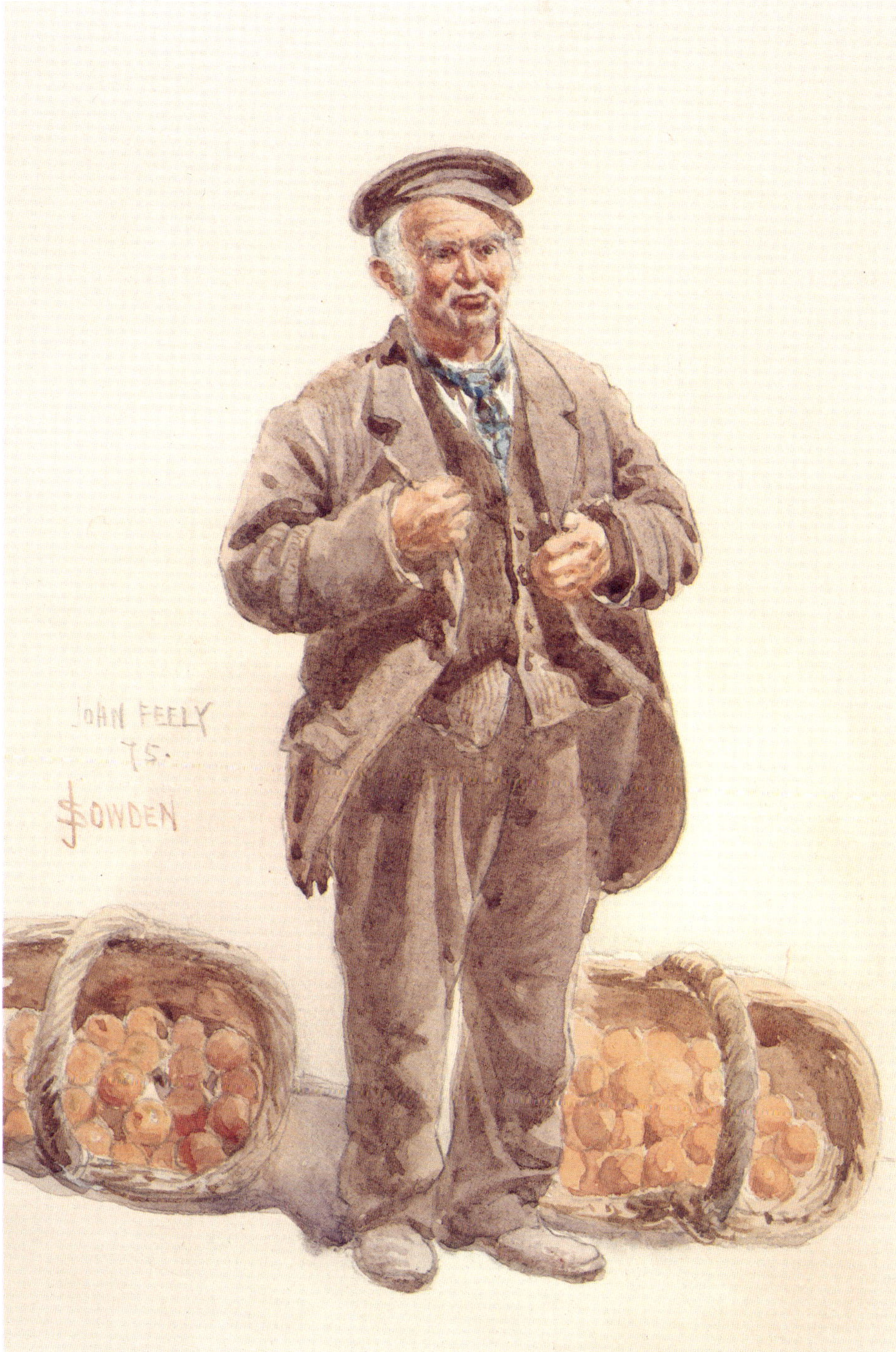
JOHN FEELY
75.
J SOWDEN

38. Edward WALTON

Perhaps Bradford's youngest negro, *Spider* Walton was only sixteen years of age when he posed for Sowden in late June 1888. He originated from Peru and sold flowers along Kirkgate and Darley Street, where his mother and father also sold flowers. His family lived in Leeds.

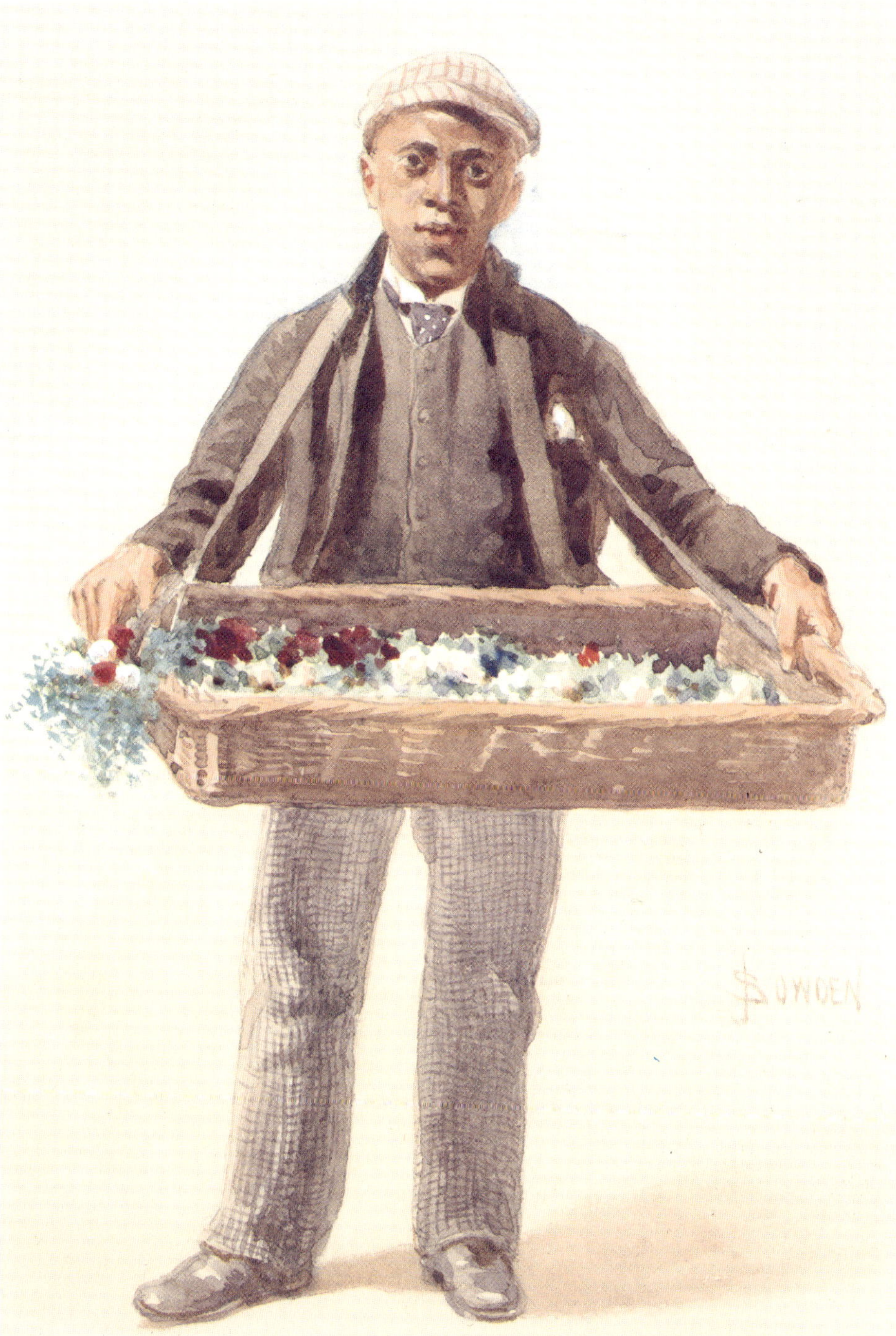
BOWDEN

39. Abraham TODD

On Tuesday 12th June 1888, two aged former textile workers successively visited the Institute studio to pose for John Sowden. In the morning the 83 year old Joseph Hill posed for his portrait. Hill was formerly a hand comber, one of that depressed class made redundant by the invention of the 'nip' machine in 1845.

In the afternoon came the severely crippled Abraham Todd, better known as *Abe Newlay.* Aged 66, he had been a mill worker since the age of 6 and it was probably standing at the spinning frames for long hours during his formative years, that contributed significantly to Abe's disability.

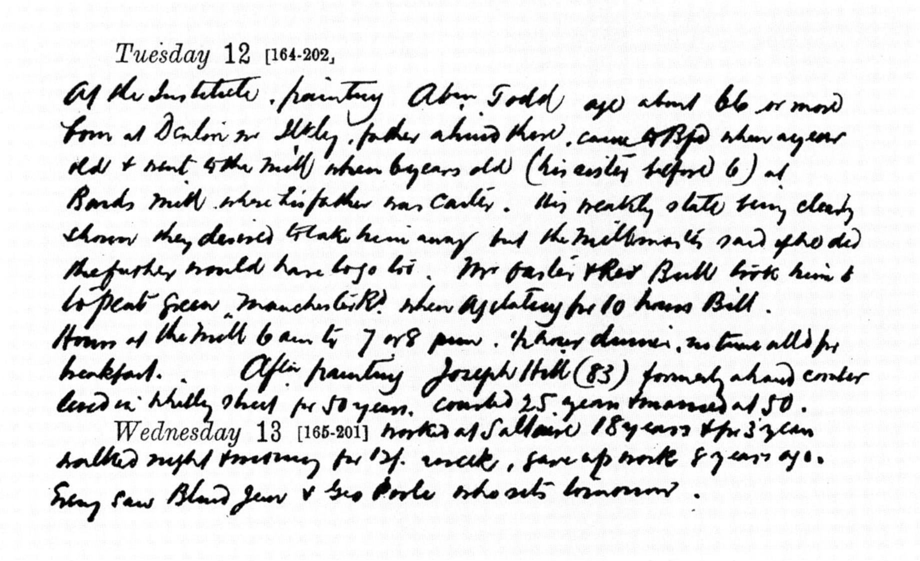

Tuesday 12 [164-202,

At the Institute. painting Abm Todd age about 66 or more born at Denton nr Ilkley, father lived there. came to Bfd when a year old & went to the mill when 6 years old (his sister before 6) at Bonds mill where his father was Carter. His weakly state being clearly shown they desired to take him away but the millmaster said if he did the father would have to go too. Mr Oastler & Rev Bull took him to Peel Green, Manchester, when agitating for 10 hours Bill. Hours at the mill 6 am to 7 or 8 pm. ½ hour dinner, no time allowed for breakfast. After painting Joseph Hill (83) formerly a hand comber lived in Whitley Street for 50 years. combed 25 years & married at 50.

Wednesday 13 [165-201]

worked at Saltaire 18 years & for 3½ years walked night & morning for 12/- week, gave up work 8 years ago. Evening saw Bland Jews & Geo Poole who sits tomorrow.

John Sowden's diary. Tuesday 12th June, 1888.

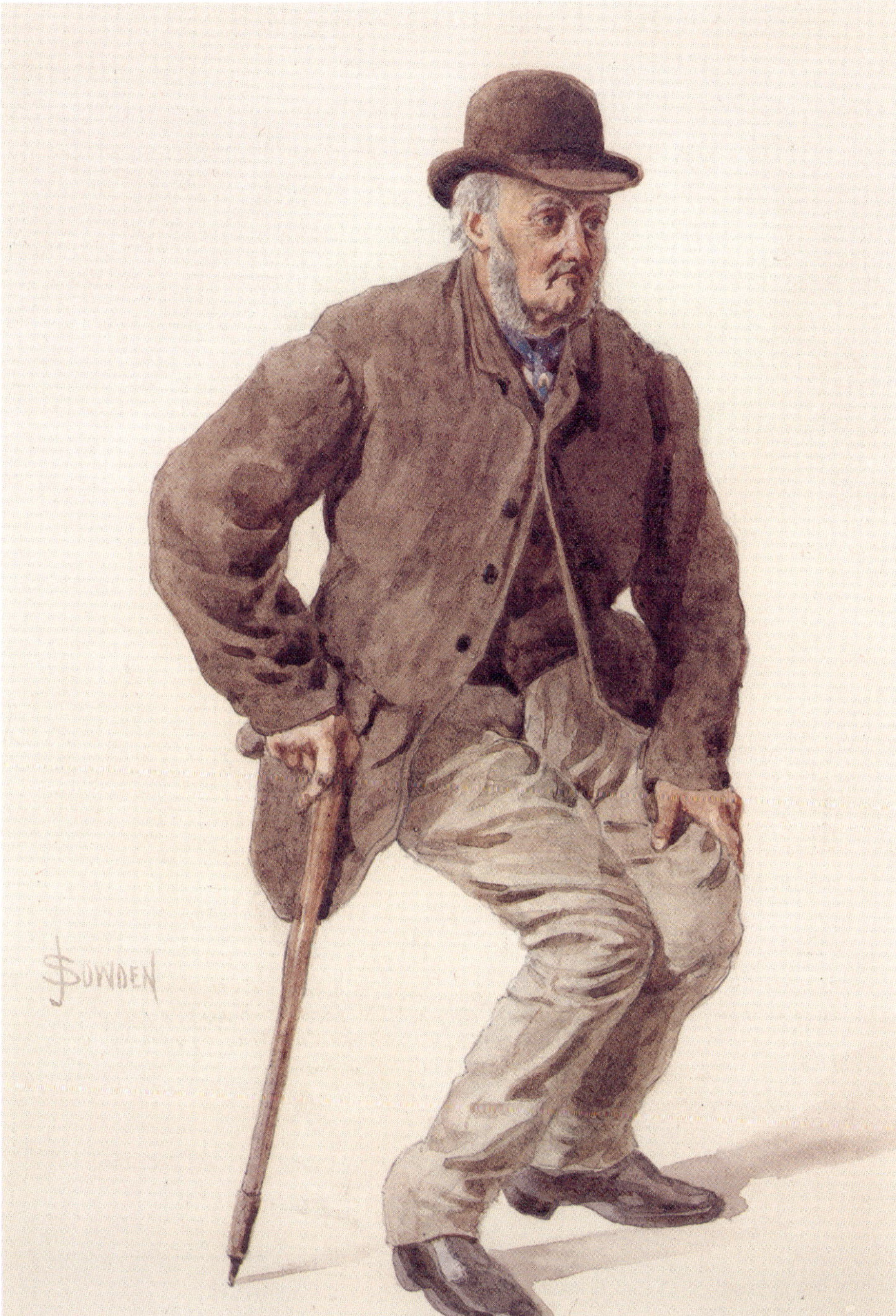

40. Harry GILMORE

Another young street hawker who should have been attending school was Harry Gilmore. Instead, Gilmore, at the age of eleven, was on the streets of Bradford selling that working class delicacy, pigs' or sheeps' trotters, lavishly laced with salt and vinegar. Gilmore's 'patch' was the market places of central Bradford.

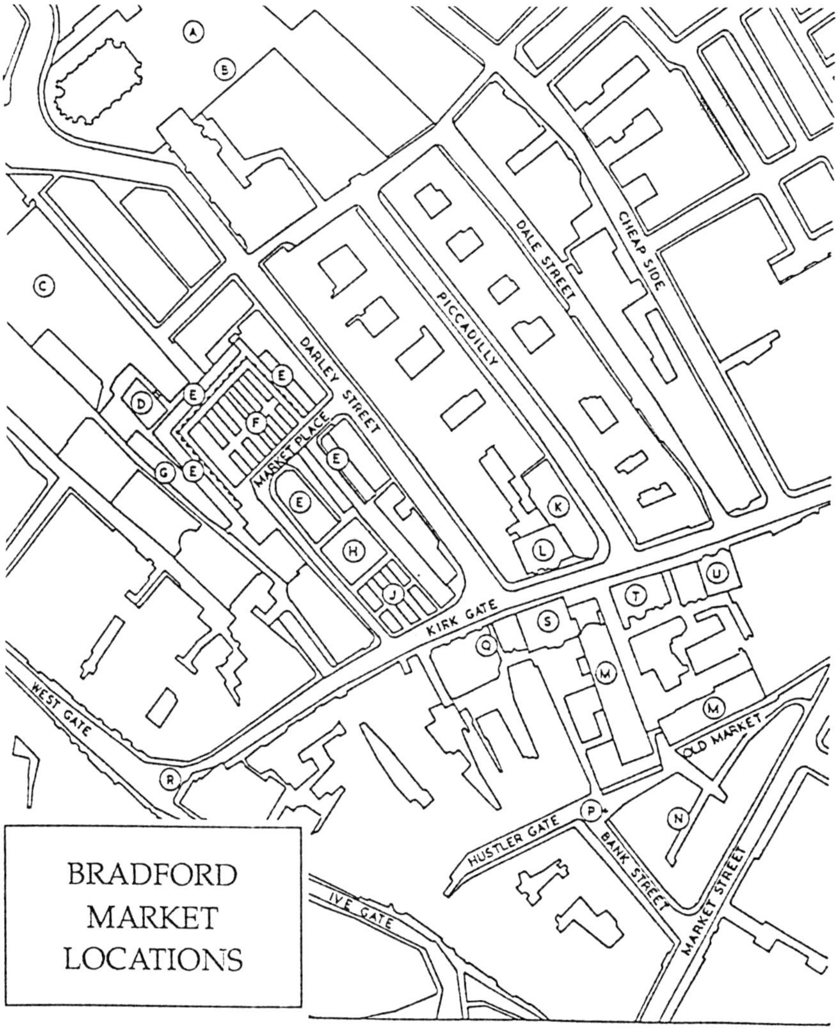

A Fair Ground
B Poultry Market
C Green Market
D Market Tavern
E The Shambles
F Fruit & Veg Market
G Slaughterhouse
H Manor House
J Fruit & Delf Market
K The Exchange
L Bradford Banking Co.
M Piece Halls
N New Piece Hall
P Remains of Old Market Cross
Q Post Office
R Old Market Place
S Talbot Inn
T Nags Head Inn
U White Lion Hotel

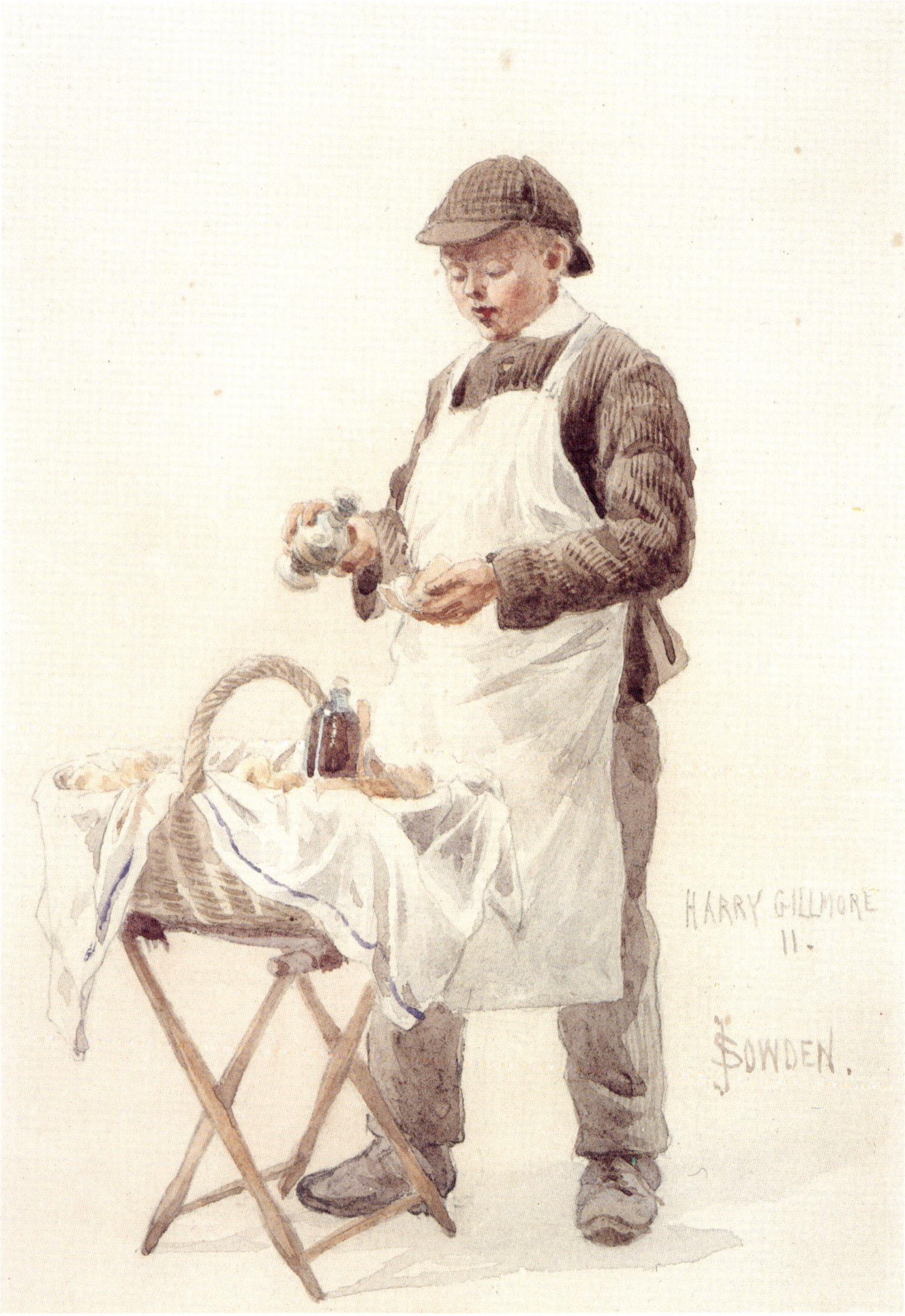
HARRY GILLMORE
11.
J SOWDEN.

41. Joseph FARNDALE

This man had the responsibility for all the foregoing characters of Bradford's streets, for Farndale was Chief Constable of Bradford. He came from very humble origins and was educated at Field House Academy in Aberford. He joined the Halifax police force working his way through the ranks to Assistant Chief Constable. In 1893 he became Chief Constable of Margate and later of York, before moving to become Chief Constable of Bradford. He later had the honour of receiving the King's Police Medal as a reward for meritorious service. Here, in all his ceremonial splendour, Farndale contrasts sharply with the everyday dress of the street characters who have gone before. However, he serves to remind us that, in addition to all the characters, Sowden also painted nearly three hundred local worthies; men and women of whom he approved and who had contributed significantly to the cultural, political and economic life of Bradford.

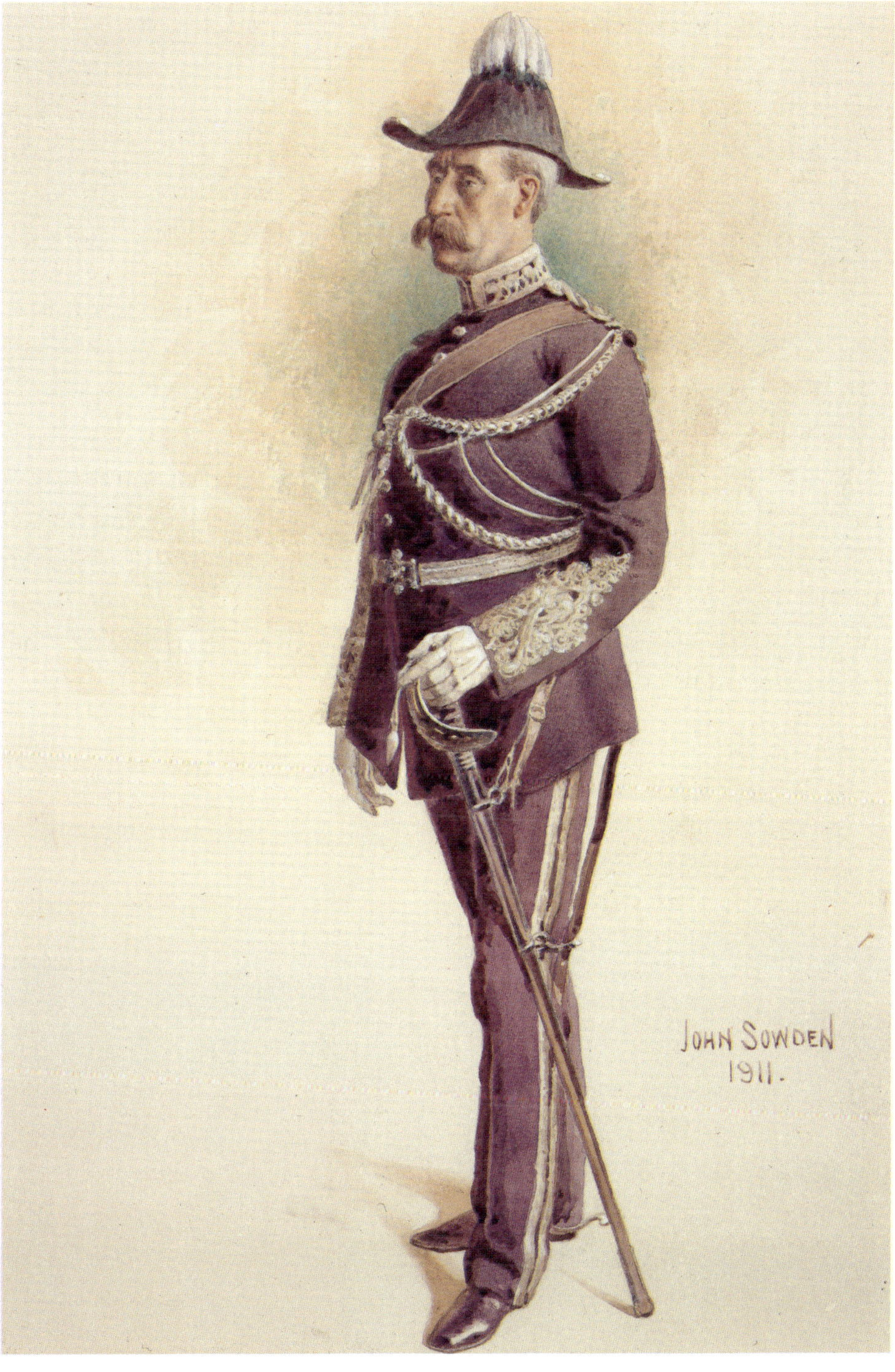
JOHN SOWDEN
1911.